THIS IS SPIRITUALISM

By

MAURICE BARBANELL

Spiritual Truth Press

www.spiritualtruthfoundation.org

The republication of this book has been funded by the Spiritual Truth Foundation, a registered charity.

Amongst its aims are the promotion of Spiritualism and spiritual healing.

First published 1959
Second edition 2001
This edition 2020

© SPIRITUAL TRUTH FOUNDATION 2020

This book is copyrighted under the Berne Convention. No portion may be reproduced by any process without the copyright holder's written permission, except for the purposes of reviewing or criticism, as permitted under the Copyright, Designs and Patents Act 1988.

ISBN 978 0 85384 108 1

Spiritual Truth Press
www.spiritualtruthfoundation.org

PREFACE

This book, which so brilliantly captures the essence of Spiritualism in the first half of the last century, was published over 40 years ago and has been out of print for close on a quarter of a century. So why has the Spiritual Truth Foundation decided to reprint it at the beginning of the new Millennium? There are two reasons.

The first is one of demand: it is a much sought-after book which deserves to be available once again to seekers of truth, even though all of the mediums referred to in its pages have now passed to the spirit realm with which they had communion.

The other is to remind ourselves, in this modern age when New Age thinking permeates our lives in a way that was unthinkable fifty years ago, that the pioneers of Spiritualism were often martyrs, scorned and vilified by those too ignorant or intolerant to examine the evidence for life after death that they were providing.

We might also reflect on why forms of mediumship that were relatively commonplace in the period covered by this book namely materialisation and direct voice communications have now almost disappeared.

Gone, but not forgotten, thanks to the lively journalistic prose of Maurice Barbanell, who was privileged to witness a tremendous range of phenomena during his time as Editor of two psychic publications.

There is, however, one story that is missing from this book. Maurice Barbanell was also a medium; the channel for a highly evolved spirit whose real identity was never revealed but who was known as Silver Birch.

Perhaps modesty prevented the author from writing about his own mediumistic contribution, or maybe it was because what was communicated through him while in trance was philosophical in content and not the "hard evidence" which is largely the theme of this book.

Nevertheless, the teachings of Silver Birch have had an enormous impact on people around the world since they were first published after World War II, and the Spiritual Truth Foundation has ensured that they remain in print. A list of these titles can be found at the end of this book.

Lastly, it is to be hoped that developing mediums will be inspired to seek to achieve the same high standards so clearly demonstrated in the accounts of mediumship in these pages.

Roy Stemman
Chairman
Spiritual Truth Foundation
October 2001

CONTENTS

Preface	3
List Of Illustrations	6
Foreword	8
Beyond The Five Senses	14
Our Lives After Death	24
Voices From Beyond	32
Segrave Proves His Survival	42
Explorer's Fate Solved	54
Séance Answer To Prayer	63
Discerning Of Spirits	72
When A Medium Is Entranced	90
Saved From Suicide	96
The Moving Finger Writes	111
Mediums Are Born	131
Sermons In Stones	151
Permanent Proofs Of Survival	161
Gifts From Beyond	166
Edgar Wallace Comes Back	179
They Cure "Incurables"	187
Dead Doctor Diagnoses	202
Defying The Law Of Gravity	215
A Spirit Signature	222
Suppressed By The Church	241
The Implications	248
Pointing The Way	261
Index	268

LIST OF ILLUSTRATIONS

1. Dr J. M. Gully takes the pulse beat of a spirit fully materialised — 36
2. A photograph of Charles Good—the man who was not there — 36
3. Queen Astrid of the Belgians materialises at a Copenhagen séance — 37
4. An enlargement of Queen Astrid, the photograph taken at the séance — 37
5. Queen Astrid as she appeared on a Belgian stamp — 37
6. Embedded in the ectoplasm emerging from an entranced medium's nostril are two miniature faces — 56
7. Enlargement of a séance photograph showing the miniature faces more clearly — 56
8. A normal photograph of Raymond Lodge — 57
9. The miniature face in the photograph identified by Sir Oliver Lodge as his son, Raymond — 57
10. A séance experiment suggested by Sir Oliver Lodge — 57
11. A sequence of seven photographs depict the whole process of materialising a spirit form — 103
12. A piece of ectoplasm, draped over the medium's face and chest detaches itself to maintain the trumpet overhead Ectoplasm levitates the trumpet through which spirit voices were heard — 171
13. Normal photograph of Edgar Wallace — 172
14. Spirit picture of Edgar Wallace — 172

15. Spirit pictures of the Rev. C. H. Spurgeon, the famous preacher, taken in the séance room of Glen Hamilton — 186

16. Infra-red picture showing the medium, Jack Webber, lashed to his chair so that he cannot free himself — 193

17. Eight seconds later. The medium's coat has been completely removed but the knots and ropes are left undisturbed — 193

18. Ten seconds later. The coat is seen in the process of returning — 194

19. Fourteen seconds later. The jacket is now completely restored to its former position — 194

20. A spirit hand is materialised at a séance — 214

21. Two streams of ectoplasm, reaching to the floor, envelope the medium's face — 214

22. Infra-red photography records the levitation of a table — 227

23. Infra-red photography takes you behind the scenes of a séance — 227

24. A psychic portrait by Mrs Coral Polge who never saw the subject alive — 228

25. A snapshot, found afterwards, for comparison with the psychic drawing — 228

FOREWORD

WHAT are my qualifications for writing a book with this title? After all, it deals with a subject that is regarded as highly controversial, one which usually arouses deep feelings.

I am a convinced Spiritualist because life after death has been proved, beyond a shadow of doubt, to me. This is not due to wishful thinking. For thirty-seven years I have witnessed extraordinary psychic phenomena which, in my judgment, have only one explanation. They were caused by intelligences belonging to individuals who no longer animate mortal frames.

For the last quarter of a century I have been in a privileged position. As Editor of two psychic journals, I have been invited to many séances that are not usually available to ordinary inquirers. Because I have been able to publish the evidence for an afterlife, thus showing what can be obtained in the best conditions, it has been made available to me.

I began my inquiry into Spiritualism as a sceptic, with a bias towards incredulity. My mother was a deeply religious woman with an orthodox outlook. My father, however, was an atheist. From childhood onwards I constantly heard my parents discuss the pros and cons of religion, without reaching unanimity. The years of dissension had the effect of making me first of all an atheist and later, in my teens, an agnostic. My outlook was unashamedly materialistic. My ambition was to carve out a successful commercial career and make a fortune. Fate, however, had other plans.

Thirty-seven years ago I was secretary of a literary

debating society at which famous authors were usually the speakers. It was one of my functions to ensure that we had a good discussion by opening the debate and always opposing the speaker, irrespective of what he said. I followed this course regularly, except on one fateful evening. Our speaker that night, instead of being a famous author, was a Spiritualist—I forget now why he was invited—who narrated his psychic experiences, outlining what seemed to him to be their implications.

The speaker sat down, and I stood up. As usual, my fellow members expected me to oppose what he had said. To their chagrin I disappointed them. Instead of advancing arguments against his speech, I asserted that on so controversial a subject no worthwhile opinion could be expressed without some personal experience as a basis. "This is a matter for investigation," I stated. "I have not investigated. Others who have inquired are better fitted to express their viewpoints, either for or against it."

When the session was over, the speaker approached me. "Were you serious in what you said?" he asked. "Ye-es," I replied.

"Will you put it to the test by making your own investigation?" was his challenge. Because I was in a dilemma and could not refuse without appearing to be foolish or frivolous, I announced myself as willing to conduct an inquiry. Moreover, I added, to stress the honesty of my agnostic outlook, I would express no opinion until six months had elapsed.

He invited me to attend a weekly séance held in a dingy tenement in the East End of London. Though, doubtless snobbishly, I was not impressed with the surroundings, I was surprised at what transpired. At the second séance a psychic phenomenon occurred for which I could find no alternative explanation other than that it was genuine. I was confronted with mediumship that was not telepathy, not the result of subconscious activity and not fraud, deliberate or unintentional.

Now, after thirty-seven years, I still regard myself as an investigator. I am familiar with all the alternatives offered as explanations of mediumship. Sometimes I think I could make a better case than the critics. Again and again I have tried to find normal explanations for the phenomena I have witnessed. It has always been my criterion that no supernormal theory should be accepted if a normal one will fit all the facts. Sometimes, it is true, I have been able to propound a theory that might fit one phenomenon. Then I have discovered that an intelligence which could not emanate from this world was at work behind the scenes. I was confronted with other phenomena which made complete nonsense of the theory I had advanced.

The happenings in the séance room are all pieces of a jigsaw puzzle that make a pattern only by accepting that they occur through intervention of supernormal intelligences. I do not use the word "supernatural", for I do not believe there is anything greater than natural law. All happenings, psychic or otherwise, are due to the operation of universal laws.

A fascinating example of supernormal activity is the fact that, on many occasions, I have received spirit messages through different mediums, each confirming what has been said through the other, though normally none of them could have known what had transpired at the other séances.

I have met fraud, both wilful and unconscious. I think

I can say that I have exposed more charlatans in this field than any other person. My ability to unmask the trickster has been due to the fact that I have witnessed so many genuine phenomena that I was able to recognise the counterfeit. After all, the spurious is a copy of the real. Were there no genuine phenomena, there could be no simulations of them.

My long experience, however, has shown me that the percentage of fraud in Spiritualism is exaggerated. It is no more, or less, than in any other facet of human activity. The idea that it has great prevalence is caused by Spiritualists like myself always insisting that the widest possible publicity should be given to fraudulent mediums.

In the "bad old days", when newspapers would publicise only the tricksters at séances, and largely ignore all the genuine occurrences, the impression became current that the whole of Spiritualism was riddled with cheats who battened on the bereaved. Now, largely due to the public testimony of men and women famous in all walks of life, the position is changed. Editors realise, as they have frequently told me, that, in their own parlance, Spiritualism "is a good story". They are eager to print the facts.

I write this book for the same reason that all my adult life has been spent in addressing public meetings in every large town in this country, in the U.S.A., Canada and on the Continent, and in contributing articles to national newspapers and journals published at home and abroad. What is my reason? I have come into possession of startling facts which have revolutionised the whole of my outlook on religion and philosophy and, indeed, on life itself.

"If a man die, shall he live again?" is a question that has been asked for thousands of years. Members of every religion believe, hope or fear that they will survive death. I am certain of it. Incidentally, I cannot understand the lack of logic shown by members of orthodox religions who say it is right to hope for survival and wrong to prove it.

To me, survival is a biological fact due to the operation of a natural law. Our birth is caused by the operation of one natural law, in which we have no say. If our wishes could have been solicited, and granted, how many of us would have wanted to be born? Similarly our life after death is part of the operation of another natural law, in which, again, we have no choice.

Survival is not a reward or a punishment for our actions on earth. We must continue to exist beyond the grave simply because we have no alternative.

To me the "dead" are as real and vital as what are called the living. They communicate with me regularly. I am conscious of their love, affection, inspiration, support and guidance.

As a Spiritualist minister I have conducted many funerals. There has never been any mention of mourning for those who have died—only for loved ones left behind, who have to endure the physical loss. Always I have stressed the note of triumph and gratitude that an individual has been liberated from earthly bondage into a fuller, richer and larger life.

Because my experiences have produced so profound a revolution in my own life, and given me a greater understanding of the universe and its purpose, I am willing to share my knowledge with those who are prepared to receive it.

I warn you that it may be a long search, but it is an exhilarating spiritual adventure. Even among the dross the gold is there, waiting to be found. But the treasure, when excavated, is enduring. A lengthy experience has proved to me that Spiritualism illumines the gloom, provides comfort in the hour of bereavement and strength in times of weakness, and supplies a real faith, based not on blind credulity but on certain knowledge.

If you are satisfied with your religious, philosophical, ethical and moral outlook, I cannot help you. Millions, however, in a world filled with doubt, dread and dismay, no longer accept conventional beliefs simply because they are traditional. The awesome advance of science, with its massive discoveries, for good or ill, in an atomic age, has compelled the majority to re-examine the fundamentals of their faith. Too many have discovered that orthodox beliefs no longer satisfy. They were exploded with the first atom bomb dropped at Hiroshima. Ever since, they have asked vital questions concerning man's origin, fate and purpose, for which they cannot find the answers.

This book is an attempt to supply some of them. You will read my experiences, and what seem to me to be their inescapable conclusions—that man is a spiritual being with a spiritual heritage and with a spiritual destiny to fulfil.

Chapter One
BEYOND THE FIVE SENSES

MEDIUMSHIP is the unique contribution that Spiritualism has to offer. It provides the foundation of evidence from which everything else in Spiritualism follows. It is, in my view, the basis of demonstrable fact which the honest inquirer can ascertain for himself.

I do not mean this in the sense of a scientific experiment which can be repeated again and again under individually controlled conditions. That is not possible because mediumship involves the use of human beings. Wherever you deal with human beings, the human factor can be wayward and liable to upset the most intricate calculations.

Nevertheless, through mediumship it is possible, as I have done, to receive consistently communications which prove the existence of an afterlife.

Mediumship is sensitiveness, the ability to register vibrations, radiations or frequencies which cannot be captured by any of the five senses. Wonderful though these sensory organs are, they are limited in their range of reception. The eyes will capture vibrations of light only within a certain margin. Similarly the ears will receive waves of sound only within a restricted field. From the infrared to the ultraviolet there are numerous vibrations of light which are lost to our eyes simply because they travel too quickly or too slowly. Sounds that move too rapidly or too sluggishly cannot be detected by our ears.

Man has constructed a variety of instruments which

enable him to be aware of sights and sounds that are otherwise lost to his senses. The telescope reveals the majesty of the heavens that the eye cannot see. The microscope enables us to be familiar with minute forms of life which are beyond our vision. Radar, X-ray, radio and television capture for us vibrations that are beyond the range of our visual and auditory organs.

The medium is, in effect, a human radio or television set. He or she—it is usually a she because women are more sensitive than men—is able to tune in to a world of activity that for the rest of mankind is invisible and inaudible. Just like the radio or television set, every medium is limited in her range of reception. Unlike their mechanical counterparts, however, mediums can, by development, increase their capacity for reception.

What is it that the clairvoyant sees, and what is called the clairaudient hears? Death merely means a change of wave-length for those who die. They discard their physical bodies, when the passing is normal, just as we dispense with an overcoat when the cold weather has gone. In their new state they express themselves through the spirit bodies that they always possessed. These, very largely, are replicas of the material bodies, except that they do not reproduce disease, infirmity or old age.

This has been perfectly expressed in the beautiful language of the New Testament when Paul says: "There is a natural body and a spiritual body." That is followed by the statement: "For this corruptible must put on incorruption and this mortal must put on immortality."

In dying, people are not transferred to another universe, for there is no removal in a geographical sense. There is only one universe, as, indeed, there is only one life, with an infinite number of manifestations. Each gradation merges into the next. In reality it is wrong to speak of an afterlife, or even of a spirit or spiritual world. We are now as much in the spirit world as ever we will be. We are no nearer it in an aeroplane, or farther from it in a submarine.

The dead—a cold, unattractive word which contradicts the reality—are still in the same universe as we are. I have heard spirit communicators say that we are the dead and they are the living. They cannot manifest their presence to us because we are spiritually deaf and blind. As they have parted with their physical bodies, they cannot reach us through our five senses. Just as we have to use instruments and appliances to register what our eyes and ears cannot receive so we have to utilise the services of a medium to achieve spirit communication.

The blind man cannot see the setting sun. The deaf man cannot hear the song of birds. Nevertheless, the sunset is there, and birds do sing, as those with normal sight and hearing know to their joy.

The medium tunes in to those on her wavelength and registers what she "sees" and "hears". Neither the "seeing" nor the "hearing" involves utilising eyes or the ears. The process is subjective, not objective, though when excellent attunement is attained, and reception is brilliant, the result appears to be objective.

Mediums whom I have questioned on the technique of communication explain that it is as if they have an inner radio or television set. Clairvoyants tell me that their vision is in no way affected if their eyes are tightly closed. Clairaudients obviously do not hear voices in their communications, simply because the communicators no longer speak with voices.

Mediumship involves the use of the faculties of the spirit body which we all possess and which we will utilise when we die. These faculties of the psyche are either dormant or nearer the surface. When they are nearer the surface you have the potentialities of mediumship, which then have to be developed. In that sense mediumship is a gift with which the person is born. Mediums are born, and then have to be developed.

In earlier civilisations, when the denizens of this globe lived closer to nature than we do, their psychic faculties operated more readily. These, alas, have become stifled by the growing complexities of modern civilisation which impose an artificiality of existence for most of mankind.

Psychic faculties can be exercised without the use of mediumship, Telepathy is one obvious example. The gifted fortune-teller is utilising psychic faculty. Intuitions, hunches, premonitions, forebodings, these are all examples, in my view, of psychic powers in operation. They produce results for which at the time there are no normal explanations. Space and time are conquered in flashes which belong to non-physical faculties.

Mediumship comes into being when these innate psychic powers are developed in conscious co-operation with what are called spirit guides, who are qualified, because of their advanced evolutionary state, to act as tutors in spiritual matters.

Broadly, mediumship falls within two categories, mental and physical, though sometimes they merge into one another. In the mental field there are clairvoyance (clear seeing), clairaudience (clear hearing), degrees of trance ranging from stages of control to complete unawareness of what is being said, and automatic writing which can culminate with the communicator reproducing his individual traits and mannerisms.

In the trance states it is mostly the guide who speaks, utilising the medium's vocal organs—in rarer cases an artificial larynx is temporarily constructed and a guide speaks in a totally different voice. When trance mediumship has reached its highest quality it is possible to get direct control by communicators other than guides.

The physical phenomena have many varieties. In direct-voice séances the communicator speaks in a temporary reproduction of his old earthly voice. This can be so remarkable that it is possible to detect individual intonations.

In spirit photography there appears on the plate or film an "extra" which is an excellent reproduction of the communicator's features, even though, sometimes, no precisely comparable photograph was ever taken on earth.

With materialisation, the rarest of all phenomena, the manifesting entity builds a temporary duplicate of his physical body, a reproduction that is the greatest marvel of the séance room.

All these physical phenomena involve the use of a substance called ectoplasm, which the medium possesses in invisible form. The word "ectoplasm" (from the Greek ektos and plasma—exteriorised substance) was originated by Dr Charles Richet, a French professor of physiology, after witnessing it streaming from mediums on numerous occasions. Baron A. von Schrenck Notzing, a German physician who specialised in psychiatry, spent thirty-five years in research and conducted hundreds of séance experiments. Occasionally, he obtained permission to amputate portions of ectoplasm for chemical and microscopic analyses. He gives the chemical analysis as: "Colourless, slightly cloudy, fluid (thready), no smell; traces of cell detritus and sputum. Deposit, whitish. Reaction, slightly alkaline." Under the heading of "Microscopic Examination", he gives the following: "Numerous skin discs; some sputum-like bodies; numerous granulates of the mucous membrane; numerous minute particles of flesh; traces of `sulphozyansaurem' potash. The dried residue weighed 8.6o gr. per litre; 3 gr. of ash."

Ideoplastic by nature, ectoplasm is capable of being moulded to "manufacture" the equivalent of the human body. Its relationship to materialisation is similar to that of protoplasm in all material forms of life. Though nonmaterial in its primal state, ectoplasm is somehow compounded by "spirit chemists" until it assumes the equivalent of the human body, with a pounding heart, pulse beats and warm, solid hands. It becomes a form that breathes, walks and talks, and is apparently complete even to fingernails.

The medium plays a vital part in these manifestations. There is a cord, albeit invisible, connecting the medium and the materialisation, performing much the same function as the umbilical cord. The "miracle" of materialisation is that in a few minutes there is reproduced in the séance room the birth which normally takes nine months in the mother's womb. And, even more striking, in these few minutes there will appear an individual showing himself, say at the age of sixty, when he died.

A form of mediumship which has achieved great

prominence is spirit healing. Here the human instrument becomes the channel for a spirit power which demonstrates its reality by achieving cures often in cases where "incurable" has been the dreaded medical verdict. The medium's development, once he recognises the possession of his gift, consists of learning, by constant practice, to become the vessel for the greatest possible degree of spirit power to be poured through him.

This is vastly different from magnetic healing, in which the healer's own vital force is used on the sufferer and a process analogous to recharging a battery occurs. It is also different from what is known as faith healing, where the patient is imbued with the idea that the acceptance of certain religious doctrines may precipitate a cure.

Though, undoubtedly, faith on the part of the sufferer helps in spirit healing, I can cite many cures that have been achieved where the patient was completely sceptical about the healer's powers. In addition, children too young to have faith have been healed by mediums. What is even more extraordinary is the fact that a tremendous amount of healing is done at a distance, and successes are obtained though healer and patient are separated by oceans and continents. Absent healing, as it is called, has triumphed in hundreds of instances where the patients did not even know that application had been made on their behalf. Obviously, in these examples, there could be no element of faith on the patients' part.

The laying-on of hands, and the prayers offered for the sick, in churches of many denominations, are forms of healing that are different from the kind practised by mediums. Sometimes it may be that the minister, even if he does not know it, is expressing a psychic gift. It is, of course, true that all healing stems from the one divine infinite source. The healing medium is characterised by the fact that he works in conscious co-operation with the spirit beings who are his guides. All the outstanding spirit healers are satisfied that they have had evidence to prove the reality of these guides, some of whom are continuing the work of alleviating suffering which they performed on earth.

Many of the cures achieved through healing mediums have been so spectacular that even medical men have described them as "miracles". They are not, however, miraculous in the sense that natural law has been suspended or abrogated. They are instances of supernormal happenings, of spirit power, akin to the life force, being able to achieve results which were medically "impossible".

Spirit healing treats the cause and not the effect, the origin of the sickness and not its symptom. It is being increasingly recognised that a large number of illnesses have a mental or a spiritual origin. These diseases are described as psychosomatic. Typical examples are that worry can produce ulcers, and a shock cause a heart attack. Mind, body and spirit are so inter-related that there is a constant interplay.

There are many modern medical men who do not hesitate to declare that fear, jealousy, greed, envy and frustration are the true causes of many diseases. Drugs cannot cure these causes. Spirit healing is particularly successful in psychosomatic illness.

Because they are clairvoyant, many healing mediums are able to give accurate diagnoses and discover the causes of illness. Their clairvoyance will sometimes confer a kind of X-ray vision on them. In other cases they are able to see the aura, the coloured emanations from every individual which surround his body like an ovoid. This human rainbow that we all possess reveals every secret to the clairvoyant gaze and indicates clearly the seat of every disease.

Dr Walter J. Kilner, of St Thomas' Hospital, London, conducted a long inquiry into the aura and recorded the results in his book The Human Atmosphere. With its first edition, published in 1911, a dicyanin screen (a solution of coal tar dye between two hermetically sealed pieces of glass) was enclosed which rendered the aura visible to normal sight. Dicyanin, which originally came from Germany, was unobtainable for years. Substitutes were not found to be satisfactory. Now that dicyanin is available in Britain once more there are opportunities for experimenters to supplement Dr Kilner's researches.

The colours of the aura denote emotion, temperament and character. Yellow indicates intellect and wisdom, deep red means anger, orange ambition, blue devotion, purple spirituality, grey fear and murky green jealousy. When clairvoyants see the aura beginning to shrivel it is a sure sign of impending death. I have frequently checked the statements made by a medium's observation of a stranger's aura and found them to be accurate.

The point I want to stress is that mediumship is the only rational explanation for the psychic phenomena I have described. It is possible to take any one phenomenon and to suggest an alternative explanation that does not involve the intervention of beings and powers from beyond this world. It is possible, for example, to say that sometimes what is called clairvoyance may be telepathy, or an unconscious form of self-hypnotism.

My long experience, based on witnessing over three thousand séances, has proved that psychic phenomena form a pattern. The pattern clearly reveals to me that at work there are intelligences who do not belong to earth. I have applied all the tests which my reason could suggest—some of them are described in the chapters which follow. And I have tried all the alternative explanations. In the end I have been forced to the conclusion that the phenomena are caused by intelligences from the spirit world. That is the only explanation which fits all the facts.

Chapter 2
OUR LIVES AFTER DEATH

THROUGH mediumship I have received communications describing what life is like in the world beyond the grave. The accounts have come from people who dwell there and who describe their first-hand experiences. There are limits to what they can tell us because of their inability to transmit complete pictures of an existence which is superphysical and is superior to earthly dimensions and limitations. Language is an artificial method which is inadequate to convey the totality of thoughts and ideas. The ideas and thoughts, being non-material, are greater than language which is material. A one-pint jug obviously cannot hold a gallon of milk.

Nevertheless from these spirit communications we obtain glimpses of the kind of life that we shall experience when our turn comes to say farewell to earth. Indeed, apart from mediumship, no detailed description of the afterlife has been presented. In the New Testament there is to be found the statement: "In my Father's house are many mansions." But nothing is said as to what the mansions are like, how they are made, or who will dwell in them.

One day after death you will be precisely the same individual as you were the day before, except that you will have discarded your physical body. You do not have to die to become a spiritual being. You are a spiritual being today. Death comes when the real you withdraws itself and functions through your spirit body.

Life in the spirit world is not hazy, unsubstantial or

nebulous, but full of activity. There are ample opportunities and occupations for everybody. It is both foolish and erroneous to imagine that when we pass from this life we sleep for ever, or until such time as there will be a resurrection. Death is resurrection.

People are accustomed to think of the material world as being real and solid. But solid matter is very much an illusion. Nuclear fission has made us all painfully realise that energy and reality are to be found only in the invisible.

To the vast majority the things of the mind or the spirit are shadowy and vague. But to those who live in the Beyond the spiritual and the mental are real and the physical is the shadow. Our thoughts and aspirations are more tangible to them than our so-called solid walls.

It is all a matter of comparison. While we dream, for example, all the events that occur appear to be actual happenings. If dreaming were to be our perpetual existence, then all that occurs in that state would be as tangible and as solid as our surroundings appear to be on earth. It is only when we awaken, and our five senses function, that we dismiss the dream-world happenings as nebulous, simply because we are now functioning in a different dimension.

There may be, after death, for many people a period of rest and recuperation to enable them to adjust themselves to the new life. The sad fact is that most individuals are so ignorant of spiritual verities that it is a tremendous shock to them to find they have survived the grave. In a minority of cases it may take the equivalent of hundreds of years for individuals to awaken after their passing. These are the earthbound ones so often responsible for hauntings, whose spiritual natures seldom functioned because of their selfish or greedy lives.

Though death has freed them from their physical bodies, their lack of evolution still chains them to earth, even though they are in a spirit world. Some of them are responsible for obsessing drug addicts and dope fiends and are also the cause of a great deal of insanity, which, incidentally, can be and has been cured through mediumship. In many of these cases the obsession is an unconscious act on the part of the intruding spirit entity. Dr Carl Wickland, a distinguished American medical man, prints authenticated cases of such cures in his book Thirty Years Among the Dead. By giving an electrical shock to the victim, the obsessing entity was dislodged and controlled the medium, who was the doctor's wife.

It does not take long, however, for the average person with his mixture of homely virtues and trivial "vices" to adjust himself. Fortunately there are relatively few really wicked people, as, unfortunately, there are relatively few saintly individuals.

The overwhelming majority of mankind has nothing to fear from death. Usually, on awakening, the newcomer is greeted by loved ones who have preceded him. Families are reunited, friendships renewed and old associations re-established. Recognition presents no problem. Those who love us in the larger life have constantly watched over us and usually help when it comes to our passing. Because in the spirit world thought is a reality, they are able to show themselves as we knew them.

Once the readjustment due to shock has been made, we discover that we are not in a strange world. The truth is that we have already visited it on thousands of occasions.

We "die" every night. Our separation from our physical body is temporary merely because the connecting cord is not severed. Just as the umbilical cord has to be cut before we can achieve our entry into this world, so the "silver cord" attached to the spirit body has to be severed before we can make our exit from earth.

When we sleep, our spirit body departs and travels in that larger domain which is destined to be our permanent existence. Though we are now unconscious of these spiritual excursions, and of the many stimulating experiences we enjoy, they become known to us by association of ideas after, we pass on. What were stifled memories, incapable of expression on earth, are now released into complete awakening.

One great factor that operates is the immutable law of attraction. Only those of like spiritual qualities can dwell on the same plane in this new life. A husband and wife, who were joined only by a legal tie, between whom no love existed and who were mentally divorced from one another, will not be together in the spirit world.

People often ask who will be the constant partner of a thrice-married man when they all have passed on. The problem, however, will not even arise. There are no sexual jealousies Over There. Real love, and parallel spiritual and mental attainment, provide their own solution. There can be no incompatibilities, no putting a face on things, no hypocrisy, no keeping up pretences to satisfy convention. Sooner or later affinities meet— and this is the real spiritual marriage —when divine justice is achieved and compensation is made.

I have frequently heard a spirit message from a wife

expressing satisfaction at her husband's choice of a partner for his second marriage. This is an example of what I mean when I say there is no sex jealousy on the part of evolved beings in the Beyond. I have also occasionally listened to spirit messages in which the communicating husband or wife has warned his or her partner of the undesirability of the marriage that was being contemplated.

I know that many readers will find it hard to understand, but in the Beyond people do live in houses, though these are not made of bricks and mortar. They are constructed out of thought, which is the most malleable of substances in a world where thought is the reality. It is as tangible to beings in a spirit world as bricks and mortar are to us.

A similar principle applies to the clothing that is worn, although this does not slavishly follow earthly fashion, but consists of robing, which provides an index of the individual's spiritual attainment. The fundamental instinct to clothe oneself persists in the spirit world where mental states are realities.

In its lowest levels people eat and drink, so long as they think it necessary to do so. They obtain the illusion which, of course, is real to them, of what they require. And it satisfies them until they progress to higher levels where they know this kind of sustenance is unnecessary.

Unlike our world, there are no language problems in the afterlife, for nationality does not persist. Thought is the only language, and telepathy the means of communication. Deception, pretence, cheating and lying are impossible. There are no secrets. Every individual is known for what he is, mentally and spiritually.

There is no age in the physical sense, but a growth

towards spiritual maturity. Thus children grow "older" as they evolve, while old people grow younger in spirit.

Labour consists of pursuing occupations in which people express natural gifts and talents. On earth, economic and other factors often prevent these gifts from finding expression and there are millions of square pegs in round holes. In the Beyond there are endless opportunities for evolving these talents—halls of music, learning, culture and education. The teachers include those whose accomplishments brought them earthly fame.

For countless women who had maternal yearnings which they could not satisfy, spirit life will indeed be a heaven, for their longings will be fulfilled in caring for children who have preceded their parents.

There is no money to be earned, no property to buy, no cars to acquire, no rent to pay, but ample opportunities for expressing the real self in service.

There are no poor and rich in the Beyond, except poverty and richness of spirit. Spirit life is one of continuous progress in which every individual gradually eliminates the dross from his nature in his striving towards perfection. There is no heaven or hell in the theological sense. These, however, are real mental states which we have created by the way we have lived our lives.

The spirit world has no separate geographical location from earth. It is part of the one universe. It is not divided into separate, self-contained spheres or planes. Each phase blends into the next, and the process is infinite. When we die we gravitate to the spiritual sphere for which we are fitted by the character we have evolved as a result of our lives. We cannot occupy a higher sphere than the one which our spiritual status determines. Nor will we desire to occupy a lower one, unless it is for a specific purpose, such as to perform labour of a truly missionary character.

After death, to put it simply, the saint and the miser do not dwell on the same plane. Spiritually, each is what he has made himself to be, by his actions, words and thoughts.

There are both compensation and retribution, because the natural laws of cause and effect are perfect in their operation. There is no Great Judge on a white throne, separating the sheep from the goats, for we have "judged" ourselves in the spiritual nature we have attained by the character we have formed. That is our spiritual passport. Our character, for which each normal individual is responsible, is moulded by our earthly lives.

The overwhelming majority will not find anything to disappoint them beyond the grave. Indeed, there will be much to give them cause for rejoicing. Their worst enemy is the ignorance which makes them unprepared for the life that follows death.

Heaven will be the reward of a life wisely spent on earth. This will enable individuals automatically to be with those they truly love, provided that there is a similarity of spiritual status, and with friends having a common mental affinity and affection. Hell will be a self-inflicted punishment for a selfish life which compels the individual to dwell with those of a like nature to himself.

One of the greatest temporary sorrows in the spirit world is the vast number of people who cannot make themselves known to loved ones left behind who are mourning them. This, as I have realised many times, is a pathetic spectacle, as they make desperate efforts to communicate through strangers to reach these grief-stricken ones. In time, taught by wise teachers, they adjust themselves. Some of them labour to destroy the earthly ignorance which created a barrier between the two states of existence. As they become accustomed to their new life, they fit themselves into their proper place and learn to use their talents.

There is no idleness, no laziness and no unemployment. Because there is no physical body there are no ravages to repair. Travel presents no problem, for all locomotion is speedily accomplished as the thought desires it.

Some of the spirit world's denizens are engaged on tasks which entail conscious or unconscious co-operation with people on earth. In the arts they seek to inspire all who are receptive. Scientists, inventors and pioneers are constantly at work attempting, often successfully, to inspire like minds in our world.

Chapter 3
VOICES FROM BEYOND

THE most convincing and sustained evidence of the afterlife that I have received has come to me at direct-voice séances. Though I have read all the worth-while literature in Spiritualism produced in the last hundred years, I have not come across any accounts to excel the proofs received in the séance room of Estelle Roberts, one of the world's greatest mediums and the possessor of nearly every psychic faculty.

There, once a fortnight, it was my privilege to be present when dramatic reunions between the living and the so-called dead were enacted. At their best, and this was a frequent occurrence, these conversations were so natural that it was hard to believe that one of the two participating voices I heard emanated from a speaker across the gulf of death.

The spirit voices came through what was called a trumpet, though it was really a megaphone in the shape of a cone, and made out of tin. These séances were always held in pitch darkness at the request of the medium's spirit guide.

When I asked whether he could obtain the result if the room had a faint illumination, his answer was: "You give me my conditions and I will produce the evidence." He certainly fulfilled his promise, as I shall describe.

I should explain that darkness, or a ruby light, is usual for this form of psychic phenomena and for materialisation. The guides responsible for these results say that the process involved is akin to the germination of life, which always requires darkness.

Spirit voices can sometimes be produced in ordinary light. I heard this phenomenon at a spontaneous and unexpected demonstration when I was in America. As part of my lecture tour, I had reached Lily Dale, New York, which is America's largest Spiritualist camp. It is not, as you might infer from this description, a collection of tents. It is a small town with two hotels which, in the summer months, becomes the Mecca of thousands interested in Spiritualism. Nearly all phases of psychic phenomena are demonstrated by as many as sixty or seventy mediums. There is an auditorium which holds two thousand people.

On the day of our arrival, a tea party was given in honour of my wife and myself. To it were invited all the mediums then staying in Lily Dale. It was a brilliant summer afternoon, with sunlight streaming through the windows. There was a hubbub of conversation, as is usual when seventy or eighty people are having tea. Many of them were smoking.

Yet in these surroundings, which I would have regarded as being unfavourable to psychic phenomena, I had an outstanding experience. My wife was introduced to a stranger, a medium named Mrs Ann Keiser, who had come from Buffalo. I must stress that this was their first meeting.

Unexpectedly, a third voice broke into the conversation and announced itself as belonging to my wife's dead grandmother. She gave her name and mentioned that my wife had been named after her. This statement was correct and was one which the medium could not have known, seeing that the grandmother had died in Britain. I say this confidently because even I did not know that my wife had been named after her maternal grandmother. She had died when my wife was three years old.

Next came the equally audible spirit voice of my wife's dead brother, a victim of the First World War, who also gave his name and said: "I have been waiting for this opportunity to talk to you." My wife came to me to describe this unexpected happening.

I took Mrs Keiser into an adjoining room, where there was less noise, wondering whether the demonstration would be repeated. At first there was a sibilant whisper, which gradually became louder, until my dead brother-in-law was speaking quite distinctly and in a masculine voice. All that he said was of a highly evidential nature, referred to matters which had arisen since I left England and answered some questions which were in my mind, though the medium knew nothing about them.

The spirit voice, so far as I could tell, came from the region of the medium's solar plexus. All the time that the voice was speaking, Mrs Keiser's lips were tightly closed. This was a phenomenon that could not be explained away by ventriloquism. And it was certainly not the medium's voice.

A few days later, I had more examples of this solar-plexus voice mediumship when I shared the platform at Lily Dale with T. John Kelly who, though he was born in South Wales, has lived in Buffalo for most of his life. It is a curious fact that nearly all mediums possessing this psychic gift either lived in Buffalo, or in that region of the Niagara Falls, or else developed the gift in that locality. It may be that there is some connection between the energy released by the cascading waters and the unfolding of this form of voice mediumship.

The first time I spoke in public at Lily Dale, Kelly was the medium who followed with a psychic demonstration.

Its purpose was to answer, while he was securely blindfolded, questions written by the audience and placed in sealed envelopes.

He was seated next to me on the platform. In broad daylight I heard a spirit voice, coming from the region of his solar plexus, address me by my nickname. It began as a whisper, gradually becoming louder until the words could be distinctly heard.

Kelly's successful demonstration consisted of "reading", sometimes without even opening the envelopes, the written questions and then giving the answers. But it was not he who spoke. The voice which came through his lips, while he was said to be entranced, was that of an individual who claimed to be his dead father. Not having known Kelly's father, I cannot say that it was his voice, or a replica of it. I can say that it was not the medium's voice. What made the proceedings, which lasted almost an hour, all the more remarkable, was that I heard the voices of people, who said they were dead relatives of members of the audience, give the answers to the questions, and Kelly's father repeated them. I heard this phenomenon several times during my week's stay in Lily Dale. Frequently, when I spoke to Kelly, though the medium was not in trance, his father's spirit voice would take part in our conversation. It always seemed to emanate from the region of the medium's solar plexus.

There must be something in the climatic conditions of America which is propitious for this type of mediumship. Kelly, and other American Spiritualists, were my fellow passengers in the ship going to Britain. Midway in the Atlantic Ocean we held a public séance, which attracted nearly two hundred people.

Dr. J. M. Gully, of the Royal College of Surgeons, takes the pulse beat of a spirit fully materialised in the laboratory of Sir William Crookes, one of the greatest chemists of his day. Sir William took the picture. The seance was held under test conditions imposed by the scientist, who listed the differences in colouring, hair, height, heart-beat, etc., between the medium and the materialisation.

The arrow indicates the face of a man who was not there—Charles Good the only absent member of the first Legislative Council of British Columbia. When this photograph was taken before the Council met on January 13th, 1865, Mr. Good was seriously ill and reported to be dying. No one was more surprised than he when, on recovering, he saw his face in the photograph. The original photograph hangs in Parliament Buildings in Victoria B.C.

(Courtesy of Provincial Archives)

Queen Astrid, wife of King Leopold of the Belgians, materialises at a Copenhagen seance after she was killed in a car crash. Simultaneous photographs were taken by three cameras with a white flash by Pastor Martin Liljeblad, a member of the State Church. The seance was held in red light, the medium being Einer Nielsen.

An enlargement of the Queen in the photograph above.

Queen Astrid as she appeared on a Belgian stamp.

Kelly gave his psychic demonstration of answering questions in sealed envelopes, entranced as usual, and with his father's spirit voice speaking through his lips. He repeated these answers as given to him by the voices of communicators claiming to be deceased relatives or friends of the questioners. I noticed, however, that the voices were weaker in volume.

After we arrived in England, I heard the solar-plexus spirit voice of Kelly's father speak many times, but it was almost a whisper. Once, in my office, when I was directing Kelly to his hotel, and he seemed confused about my directions, this voice broke in to give even more precise details. The fact that it had diminished in volume from when I heard it in Lily Dale points to climatic conditions being responsible.

Every medium has a spirit guide, a role which Kelly's father performed. Usually, however, they are not related to the medium. Frequently they are Red Indians, a fact which puzzles newcomers. The answer is not far to seek. In the days of their prime, the North American Indians were masters of psychic laws, with a profound knowledge of supernormal forces and how they operated. This qualifies them, after their passing, to act as tutors and guides to their mediums.

The modern Red Indian has been "civilised" and Westernised, and natural psychic faculty has been stultified. His prototype, however, was in a vastly different category. Ernest Thompson Seton, one of the greatest experts on Red Indians, describes their enhanced psychic gifts in his book, Gospel of the Red Man.

To know many of them, as I have done through the years, is to regard them with great affection and respect. The ones who work through the best mediums are wise teachers who exude a quality that can be described as "lovableness". They are imbued with the idea of service.

These qualities are exemplified in the person of Red Cloud, the guide of Estelle Roberts. Though I have seen him only once, when he materialised as a temporary flesh-and-blood creation, I have spoken to him so many times that I regard him as an old friend, one whom I know better than many of my intimates in this world.

His voice, whether heard through the lips of his entranced medium, or independently in his voice séances—it is similar in both forms of mediumship—is entirely different from that of Estelle Roberts. His very masculine tone is low-pitched and husky. Although his command of English is good, he has a specially appealing way of pronouncing some of the vowels. An occasional transposition of a syllable often has an entertaining effect.

Once, when asked, Red Cloud gave details of his earthly life as a Sioux Indian. He explained also how he learned English as part of the equipment for his mission through Estelle Roberts.

Once a fortnight, alternating with his voice séance, he held what was known as a teaching circle. Its purpose was to propound the broader implications of the evidence which came at his séances. I have heard him lecture for over an hour in impromptu fashion, sometimes on complicated themes suggested by his hearers. This was always an educative evening. His talks revealed a versatility of knowledge far beyond the scope of his medium. She had to work too hard in her early life to have any time for cultural pursuits.

I have heard Red Cloud express a knowledge of science that enabled him to discuss the intricacies of this subject with a distinguished scientist. I have listened fascinated while he discoursed on medicine, both ancient and modern, with a doctor. He is an expert on dead empires, lost cities and on the customs of bygone times. His knowledge of past and contemporary religions is considerable. Added to all this, he would quote at length from the Old and New Testaments.

Though Red Cloud's statements produced differences of opinion, for he always welcomed controversial discussion, he never showed the slightest sign of irritation to any who disagreed with his viewpoints. Frequently, his humour was displayed in masterly repartee.

Estelle Roberts has been a very great friend of mine for over twenty-five years. I have visited her home on scores of occasions. Her whole life has been dedicated to her wonderful and versatile mediumship, which has demonstrated nearly every known psychic gift. She has found relaxation in almost her only other interest—her garden.

Her reading is chiefly confined to the periodicals which deal with Spiritualism. I know that the reading of any other kind of literature does not appeal to her. She has never expressed any interest in poetry, either of the present or past eras. Yet I have heard Red Cloud accurately repeat several applicable lines written by a modern poet whose verses are still unknown to the majority. And frequently he has recited impromptu verse which appropriately expressed his ideas. On many occasions I have been stirred as he spoke at length in beautiful and rhythmic verse.

I am quite certain that in her normal state Estelle is incapable of these feats. The sceptic could argue that she might keep her cultural pursuits a secret. If she could so deceive those who knew her intimately, she would compare with the greatest actresses of our time. The stage, the screen, or television, would provide her with far more lucrative rewards than she obtains from mediumship.

A profound humanity is one of Red Cloud's most endearing qualities. Always he exhibits a broad tolerance and a deep understanding of earthly problems and difficulties. Red Cloud's compassion is deep-seated, his disposition is gentle and kindly, and he never condemns.

Chapter 4
SEGRAVE PROVES HIS SURVIVAL

THE sitting for an Estelle Roberts voice séance followed a similar pattern every fortnight. There was its hard core of regular sitters, and the newcomers, who were never introduced to the medium. This was one of the precautions taken to ensure that results measured up to the highest possible standards of evidence. The group usually numbered about twenty people.

A few minutes before the séance began, cold water was poured through the two trumpets that were used. These were daubed with a phosphorescent material, exposed to the light before the sitting, and which remained luminous during the proceedings. The luminous paint enabled us to follow the movements of the trumpets, which behaved with a dexterity that was in itself a supernormal occurrence.

They would move round the room with lightning like speed, sometimes hitting the ceiling, or occasionally banging the floor. Then the two parts, of which each trumpet was made, would collapse. Soon an invisible force would reassemble the two sections into one, and the trumpets would go sailing merrily round the room again. They were guided with unerring accuracy; never once did they fumble, or hit any of the sitters.

Always one of the trumpets would propel itself immediately in front of the person who was to receive the communication. While the communicator spoke, the trumpet remained poised in mid-air, dropping only if the spirit speaker could not sustain the effort, or at the end of the communication. Sometimes, to show his mastery over these trumpets, Red Cloud, or one of his helpers, would "fondle" you with it—this is the only way I can describe what happened. The trumpet would generally touch you, with its broad end, from head to foot.

Before the séance began, the sounds of stertorous breathing came from Estelle Roberts, an indication that she was entering the trance state, in which she remained during the proceedings. It always seemed unfortunate that she should be unconscious of the dramatic events that occurred through her mediumship.

Usually every sitter in the circle held the hand of his neighbour, which Red Cloud said was helpful to the reproduction and flow of the psychic power he required to obtain his results. Occasionally we were told to free our hands. Then we were put on our honour not to touch the trumpets. These, Red Cloud told us, were always joined to his medium by "ectoplasmic rods" which, if broken, could endanger her health.

In a home circle which I regularly attended for some years, and where direct voice phenomena were obtained, we forgot to give this warning to a newcomer. In all innocence she touched the trumpet when she was being addressed. There was a groan from the entranced medium. The séance was brought to an abrupt end by her guide, who told us, as we soon confirmed, that she had a haemorrhage.

In Estelle Roberts's voice séances we were encouraged to indulge in normal conversation. Then one of the trumpets was seen to rise from the floor and the voice of Red Cloud was heard to exclaim: "Hold on!" This was always a signal that another communicator was ready to speak. The trumpet would slowly descend to the floor. You could tell by the way it rose whether the speaker was a new or an old hand. With newcomers, it rose slowly, as if a great effort were involved. With those who had previously communicated, the trumpet's movements were quick and precise.

Red Cloud's "Hold on!" was a signal for our conversation to end. Generally, while the communication came through the trumpet, a gramophone record was played. It was always the same disc, with selections from the musical comedy, "Rose Marie". It was strange to hear its popular refrains played as an accompaniment to intensely moving reunions between loved ones whom death had separated. When I questioned Red Cloud as to the reason for his choice of this record, he said it was purely a matter of vibration. The quick vibrations from this recording, he said, helped him to produce the direct-voice phenomena.

There was never any confusion at these séances, because Red Cloud, the perfect spirit master of ceremonies, spoke in between every communication. In a curtained-off alcove, a stenographer sat with a light shining on her notebook, to ensure that she made a verbatim record. I usually repeated, for her benefit, every word spoken by the communicators and the recipients.

In that small, upper room, I heard, at séance after séance, dozens of different voices that emanated from people no longer on earth. I listened to the voices of men, women and children. Nearly always, in the beginning, the spirit voices were feeble and halting. When communicators learned to master the technique, they spoke in ringing tones and could be clearly heard outside the room, and sometimes even in the garden below.

I was responsible for bringing Lady Segrave into that séance room at a time when she was broken-hearted with bereavement after her husband's death. Her dramatic story really has its beginning years before, at Daytona Beach, Florida, where, by breaking the world's speed record on land, the name of Henry Segrave made headlines on the front pages of newspapers all over the world. Before attempting the record, he had received, from an unknown person, a séance message which had come to a group in England. It was in the nature of a warning, and was said to have been given by a speed king who had passed on. It stated that a certain part of the car would snap when he reached a given speed. Segrave tested it at the speed mentioned, and it snapped. This message, Segrave volunteered, prevented a motoring accident that might have been fatal. His curiosity aroused, Segrave made some inquiries in Spiritualism when he returned to England. Knowing that his friend, Hannen Swaffer, the famous journalist, was a Spiritualist, the racing motorist called on him.

In Swaffer's flat, he witnessed psychic phenomena which intrigued his engineering mind. One phenomenon made a tremendous impression on Segrave. It happened when a non-professional medium was present. He was Archie Emmett Adams, the composer of "The Bells of St Mary's" and other popular songs, who was a living paradox.

Adams, more attracted to Theosophy than Spiritualism, resented his mediumship, even though he was the possessor of strong psychic powers. In Adams's presence, and in the normal lighting of the flat, or in broad daylight, Segrave witnessed, as many others have done, the extraordinary feat of

Swaffer's piano being levitated from the floor whenever the medium played a native tune he had heard in Honolulu. As it returned to the floor, the piano made a loud noise. Segrave often referred to this happening, and laughingly used to say: "The only time I was ever frightened was when I saw the piano jump in Hannen Swaffer's flat."

Not long afterwards there came the tragic fatality at Lake Windermere, where Segrave was attempting to create a new world speed record on water. The foremost racing motorist of his time, a man of charm and endearing personality, beloved by all his friends, ended his earthly career.

Thousands were shocked at the news of the tragedy. To Lady Segrave it was the greatest blow of her life. On the Sunday after his death, there were some curious happenings in Swaffer's flat. These involved the mysterious transfer of a newspaper from one room to another, and other happenings for which apparently there was no normal explanation. The significant fact about the newspaper was that it contained the last article ever written by Segrave. It made a reference to Swaffer and included a mention of the levitated piano. Wondering if these unusual events might have been due to Segrave trying to attract his attention, Swaffer wrote to Lady Segrave, describing in detail what had happened. He included in his letter, not the conventional words of sympathy offered to mourners, but the assurance, from one who had received proof, that in the hour of her trouble he felt certain her husband was very close. This was a difficult letter, because Spiritualists do not know, even when trying to offer real comfort, whether they will be regarded as intruders who may be rubbing salt into sore wounds. Lady Segrave expressed appreciation in her reply. She said she had taken the blow well, for it was only at moments that she realised her utter desolation.

Over a year later, she wrote to Swaffer again, this time to inquire whether he had received any communications from her husband. She had read a book on Spiritualism written by the famous journalist, which, she said, interested her enormously. It indicated to her, she added, that although her life seemed meaningless and futile, she might at least have the possibility of reunion to anticipate.

Swaffer showed me the correspondence and asked me to help Lady Segrave to make her own inquiry into Spiritualism. I thought her best introduction would be to attend one of Estelle Roberts's voice séances. But there was only one way to secure admission. It was to obtain an invitation from Red Cloud. He would either specifically nominate people he wanted to be present, or else you would ask whether you might bring a friend, without mentioning any name or giving any clue as to the sex or identity. Red Cloud would say "Yes" or "No". He never sought to ask who the friend might be. It seemed as if Lady Segrave was to be fortunate. For the following Friday—the séances were always held on that day—I had obtained permission to take two friends, a husband and wife. On the morning of the séance I learned that one of them was ill and so both would not come. This looked like an opportunity to take Lady Segrave. The problem was how to get Red Cloud's permission. I wanted to bring Lady Segrave without disclosing her identity, so that if she received a spirit communication its evidential value would not be impaired.

I telephoned the medium and said that the two friends I had arranged to take were unable to come. "Can I bring somebody else in their place?" I inquired.

"Have you asked Red Cloud?" was the reply.

"No," I had to confess. There was a lengthy argument. In the end, Estelle Roberts said she would trust me. She did not ask who the visitor would be, and I gave no indication. Then I telephoned Lady Segrave and invited her to the séance. To her dismay, she could not come. She had an important engagement which could not be postponed at such short notice. Naturally, I was very disappointed.

"Where is your friend?" the medium asked when I arrived. I explained that "my friend" was unable to come. I mentioned no names, not even whether it was a man or woman I had hoped to bring. I gave no clue of any kind as to her identity.

We assembled as usual in the upper room. The lights were extinguished. Soon one of the luminous trumpets moved, and the deep, sonorous voice of Red Cloud was heard welcoming us to the séance. Out of sheer curiosity I said to him: "Do you know anything about the person I tried to bring tonight?" His reply was cryptic. "You dry up and wait," he joked.

Later, Red Cloud addressed me and said the next communicator wanted to talk to me. I watched the trumpet as it slowly moved towards me. Then a voice spoke. "Barbanell," it called. "Yes," I replied, "who is that speaking?"

"Segrave," came the answer. "Thank you for trying to bring my wife." It was a startling and unexpected example of spirit knowledge. Though I had not mentioned to anyone in the séance room about my efforts to bring Lady Segrave, her husband had shown in unmistakable fashion that he knew. "It is all right, Sir Henry," I told him. "I am only sorry that she was unable to come."

With typical charm he insisted that it was very kind of me. I asked him for a message that I could convey to his wife. He told me what to say, which I later repeated to Lady Segrave when I telephoned her. It conveyed nothing to me, but she said it was important to her, and added that it was a very characteristic message.

A fortnight later I brought her to the same séance room. She was not introduced to the medium or to any of the sitters. Soon the voice of Red Cloud was heard greeting his friends. As he did so, one trumpet moved, seemingly of its own volition, round the circle. Suspended in mid-air, it paused in front of Lady Segrave. "You don't know me," said Red Cloud addressing her.

"No," she answered, "I am a stranger here."

"Oh no you are not! Good evening, Lady Segrave. I will soon bring your little man." I have heard him use that phrase many times, for to Red Cloud they are all "little men" and "little ladies". The trumpet moved away. The séance began to follow its usual pattern as spirit voices addressed members of the circle. Some came with only a greeting; others with comfort and guidance for loved ones or friends. Several of the conversations were quite lengthy.

Soon the trumpet returned to Lady Segrave, seated next to me. "D," said a voice. Later she told me that only her husband had ever called her by that nickname, a fact, I must stress, unknown to anyone present. All that I knew was that her Christian name was Doris.

Unfortunately, she became excited and tense at her husband's first spirit return, and could not speak. "D," repeated the voice. "Speak to him," I whispered. From experience I knew that the success of these voice séances depended on the response from the person addressed. My urging, however, seemed to make her more tense. The trumpet moved towards me. "You are there, Barbanell, aren't you?" the voice pleaded. "Yes, Sir Henry," I replied, "but please speak to your wife."

Again he addressed her by the same nickname. She mumbled a few words . . . and then the trumpet dropped, an indication that Segrave could not hold on to the necessary "power".

Immediately, Red Cloud's voice was heard. He addressed Lady Segrave. "I know how you feel," he said, "and your husband is just as excited. But I will help you both." When, after the séance, I asked Lady Segrave for her reaction, she answered: "It seems too good to be true."

Her husband, however, whose indomitable courage had brought him world fame, was determined not to be beaten. At the next sitting he showed that he had begun to master the technique of communication, for there was a great improvement. Evidence of his identity came with the first words to his wife: "I was with you on the fourteenth, D."

"Did you remember the fourteenth?" she asked. "Yes, your birthday," said Segrave, proving that he had not forgotten. Despite his natural excitement at returning to his wife, he displayed his unfailing courtesy by greeting me and saying: "I am trying hard to get through." I could not help laughing when he added: "I know how to drive a boat or a car, but I am hanged if I can get the run of this yet. I will get through. . . ."

He certainly succeeded. I felt as if I were an eavesdropper as I listened to his long conversation with his wife. They discussed a dozen matters which included mention of her domestic surroundings, friends and relatives. He touched on one topic, which she afterwards volunteered to me was unknown to anyone in the world except herself. I was delighted to notice that she had now lost her tenseness. "Are you with me in the car?" was her next question. "Yes," was the answer, "but do take care, D." "Why?" she exclaimed. "I am a very good driver." There was a pause, and the man who was the greatest racing motorist of his time, replied: "Yes, so was I. . . ." The whole conversation between husband and wife was so natural that by the time it had ended we all felt we were intruding. Later, discussing the séance with her, she mentioned that her husband, in humorous fashion, often used to criticise her driving.

I will not go into any further detail, except to say that at séance after séance the evidence for Segrave's survival began to accumulate. It was obvious that he was no longer a novice in the art of communication from the spirit world. Moreover, in his talks he revealed that he knew all that was happening to her. He became so adept at manipulating the trumpet's movements that he could bring it close to her ear and whisper so successfully that she could hear every word whilst I, seated next to her, could not even catch a syllable.

Once, after a long séance talk, she said to me: "The whole of his conversation was very characteristic, full of intimate details, so that I knew beyond doubt that it was my husband." Lady Segrave volunteered that her whole life was transformed by this new knowledge which brought her a radiance of outlook where formerly there was only despair.

One night she asked Red Cloud whether she could bring a friend to the next séance, taking care to mention no name, or to indicate whether it would be a man or a woman. The guide gave his consent. It was a man who came, one who was a stranger to the medium and to all the sitters. Lady Segrave, to ensure the evidential value of any communication he might receive, took the precaution of not introducing him by name. But Segrave knew who he was. "Mark," he called him.

It was the Earl of Cottenham, one of his oldest friends, and a man who had been associated with him in his racing career. And he had always called him "Mark". When I listened to the conversation between the two men, even I found it almost impossible to realise that one was dead and the other living. It all seemed so natural, and so obviously a reunion of old friends.

I told Segrave that he sounded so much happier than at the first time he returned. "Don't you realise that this has made it so?" he replied. "I did not want to leave her. We had all our earthly struggles together, and just as success came, this happened. I accepted it for myself, but not for her."

Lord Cottenham assured him that Lady Segrave was much happier now that she had found a means of talking to her husband. She was a regular attendant for months, and her husband never missed a chance of communicating with her. Soon he was giving evidence of helping newcomers to break through the sound barrier of death.

One night, Lady Segrave asked Red Cloud whether she could bring two friends to the next séance. He agreed and, as usual, no effort was made to inquire who they were. When these two visitors, a young man and woman, accompanied her the next time, none of us knew who they were. But Segrave did. He spoke to them both.

"Rod" was his greeting for the young man, who was his brother Rodney. Equally Segrave proved that he knew who the young woman was, for he called her by her name. She was his brother's wife. This was the first voice séance they had ever attended. They volunteered the statement that it was the most amazing experience they had ever had in their lives. Although Lady Segrave had often described her talks with her husband, they simply did not realise how natural these were.

The cumulative evidence reached the stage where Lady Segrave told me she had overwhelming conviction of her husband's survival. When I asked her to summarise her inquiry, she answered: "My evidence reveals his complete knowledge of my most intimate and private affairs. Again and again I have turned this evidence over in my mind, examined it critically and calmly. I have tried to explain it all away. I have asked myself the questions: 'Can it be telepathy or the subconscious mind? "Have I been deceived?' Always the evidence stood every test."

Chapter 5
EXPLORER'S FATE SOLVED

SPIRIT messages in that same séance room solved one of the world's greatest mysteries, the fate of Colonel P. H. Fawcett, the explorer who vanished in the heart of the Brazilian jungle. For a quarter of a century there had been rumours, speculations and theories. None of these was the answer to a riddle which had set thousands guessing.

Expeditions sent to locate him met with failure. No one could provide an authoritative answer to the questions: "Was he still alive?" "Was he held captive by unruly tribes?" "Had he lost his memory?" "Had he chosen to end his days living the kind of existence which, even at its best, was fit only for wild animals?"

In 1951, it was "officially" stated that Fawcett's skeleton had been found in the jungle, on the banks of the River of Death, in Central Brazil. These remains were brought to England and examined by Fellows of the Royal Anthropological Society, who declared they were not Fawcett's bones. But I had known sixteen years earlier that Fawcett had died, for he communicated in the séance room of Estelle Roberts.

Fawcett's romantic story began in the early summer of 1925. With his son, Jack, and a young Englishman named Raleigh Rimell, he led an expedition into the heart of Brazil to explore unknown territory, the central Brazilian Plateau. From the time they left the last outpost of civilisation, no word, by normal means, reached the outside world. But there were spirit messages.

Fawcett's expedition into this dangerous territory was surrounded with glamour. His object was to discover the lost city of the South American continent, believed to have been one of the chief cradles of prehistoric civilisation. Probably less is known of the interior of Matto Grosso, the scene of his search, than of any other inhabited area of similar size in the world. Even today, there are still huge tracts which no one has visited.

For years, expeditions had been chartered, some sponsored by the Brazilian Government, to find this cradle of a lost civilisation. Fantastic tales told about these mysterious regions referred to buried cities, hidden treasures, wealthy mines of gold and silver, prehistoric beasts and white Indians.

One story was told of an expedition which set out two hundred years ago in search of buried gold and silver. They were said to have reached the heart of the Central Plateau, and to have come upon an unexpected range of mountains. They climbed one crevice and found themselves on a fertile table-land. The spectacle that met their eyes filled them with astonishment. In front of them were the ruins of a huge city which had been built of blocks and stone. There was no sign of human life; it was completely deserted. They wondered whether they were gazing at the results of an earthquake. The expedition never returned. Other explorers argued whether this was one more addition to the many "travellers' tales".

Fawcett's imagination, however, was stirred by these accounts of the ruins of a lost world. In 1925 he wrote that its whereabouts were known, so far as "the general location

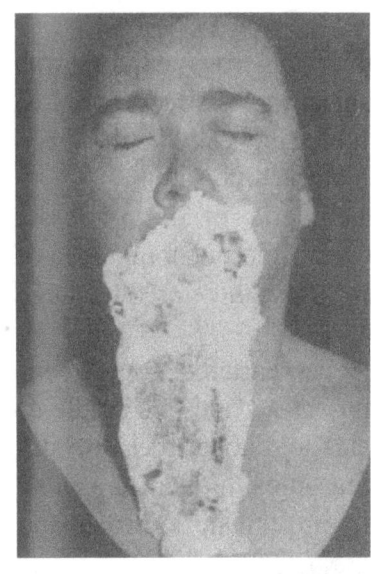

An enlargement showing the miniature faces more clearly.
(See next page).

Ectoplasm emerges from the entranced medium's nostril. Embedded in the ectoplasm are two miniature faces. This is one of a series of séance photographs taken by Doctor Glen Hamilton in his Winnipeg home. All told he used fourteen cameras with as many as twelve taking simultaneous photographs with a white flash.

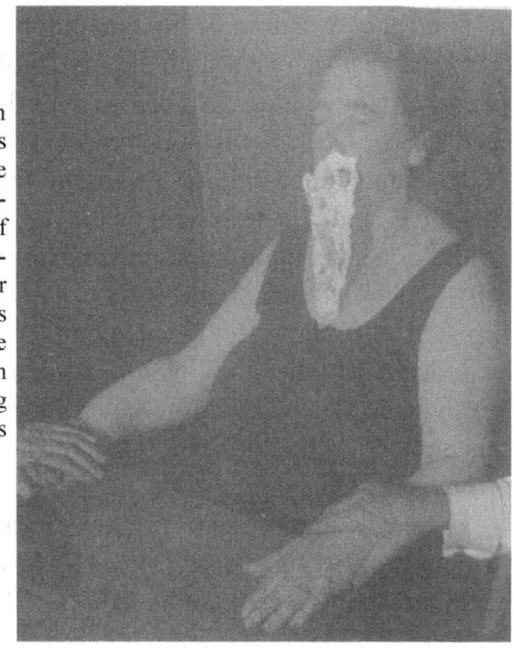

EXPLORER'S FATE SOLVED

| An normal photograph of Raymond Lodge | The miniature face in the photograph on the previous page has been enlarged. It was identified by Sir Oliver Lodge as being that of his son, Raymond, who was killed in World War I. |

A seance experiment suggested by Sir Oliver Lodge, who supplied the two solid rings, each made of a different wood. At a seance with Margery Crandon of Boston, U.S.A., the two rings were interlocked by an invisible power. So far as is known, there is no normal method of achieving this feat.

and surrounding topography are concerned", to three men. One was a Frenchman, whose last attempt to get there had cost him an eye, and he would probably make no more efforts. The second was an Englishman who, before he left the country, was suffering from an advanced stage of cancer, and was probably no longer alive. The third was himself. Fawcett, who was determined to reach his goal, was well qualified for this Herculean task. As an explorer, he had achieved world fame. He was a man of great courage, accustomed to privations, and in other dangerous expeditions had outlasted members of the party. He regarded this as his greatest adventure.

Keeping quiet about his ambitious plans, he set out on April 20, 1925, with two companions and two guides. On May 29 they reached Dead Horse Camp, where, on a previous expedition, five years earlier, one of Fawcett's animals had died. From this camp he sent a dispatch promising further messages from time to time. These he hoped to send by using a friendly Indian tribe. From the time he reached the edge of the dangerous and unknown country, nothing more was heard of the intrepid explorer. His expedition never returned. The promised messages did not come.

Fawcett's disappearance became a riddle which intrigued the world. He had expected to be absent for twenty months. When, after that time, nothing was heard of him, his friends began to wonder about his fate. Inquiries of the Brazilian Government produced the reply that their officials in the interior had failed to trace Fawcett. It was to be feared that he and his party had perished.

In 1927 a Brazilian engineer, Robert Courteville, reported that he had met Fawcett some 170 miles from the capital of Matto Grosso. Fawcett, he said, was shaking with fever and his legs were badly bitten by mosquitoes. The explorer seemed to resent Courteville's interference, so they parted. At that time, the Brazilian engineer did not know that there was any mystery concerning Fawcett's disappearance. When he was later told the facts, he said he would organise a search party and bring him back to civilisation. This expedition never materialised.

In 1928 a relief expedition was financed by an American newspaper syndicate. This was led by Commander George Dyott. They followed Fawcett's three-year-old trail, starting from Dead Horse Camp, until they came to a village of Anauqua Indians. There Dyott found a chief's son, who had swinging round his neck a small brass plate stamped with, the name of a firm which had supplied Fawcett with some air-tight cases in 1924.

The new expedition learned from the villagers that Fawcett had rested there with his two companions, both lame and exhausted. Then the explorer had moved on into unknown country. For five days, said the Indians, they saw smoke from the fires of Fawcett's expedition as it blazed its way through the tall grass. On the sixth day no smoke was to be seen. They assumed that the gallant band had been murdered. Dyott made an exhaustive search, but he could find no evidence of the suggested tragedy. He returned to civilisation unable to say whether Fawcett was alive or dead. Nothing more was heard until March, 1932, when a Swiss, named Stephan Rattin, called at the British Consulate in Sao Paulo with a strange story. Rattin, a trapper, said that a year earlier he had journeyed into the heart of Matto Grosso. There, in an Indian village, he was surprised to meet a white man he believed to be Fawcett.

Rattin described him as having blue eyes, wearing a long, white beard, and dressed in a costume of skins. He was being held prisoner by the Indian tribe and looked a sorry spectacle. Using English, a language in which he was not proficient, Rattin managed to speak a few words with the prisoner. Rattin's story was that the old man said he was a colonel in the English army, and begged him to tell a friend named Paget in Sao Paulo of his predicament. Later, it was discovered that a Major J. B. Paget had helped to finance Fawcett's last expedition.

Another significant statement made by Rattin was that the old man showed him a signet ring. When this was described to Mrs Fawcett, she said it corresponded with a ring her husband always wore. A verbatim account of Rattin's statement was given to the British Consul General in São Paulo. After a searching examination it was rejected as being too full of mistakes and inconsistencies. Besides, it was strange that Fawcett had not mentioned his companions. Three months later, Rattin set out on an expedition in the hope of finding Fawcett, but he met with no success. The mystery still remained a mystery. Leading experts declared, after examining all the facts, that in their opinion, the whole of Fawcett's expedition had perished in the summer of 1925, probably massacred by Indians. In June, 1932, in the séance room of Estelle Roberts, I was surprised to hear one of the spirit communicators talk about Fawcett.

The communicator told a friend of mine, Mrs Alice Liddell, that he wanted to confirm what he had said at an earlier séance about Fawcett being a prisoner. The explorer, he added, was mentally well, but physically ill. I asked Mrs

Liddell whether she had received any previous communications regarding Fawcett. "Yes," she replied, and told me these facts.

She was a friend of Mrs Fawcett. Two years earlier, at one of these voice séances, she had been told that Fawcett had found the lost city. In 1933 Mrs Fawcett had a séance with Estelle Roberts. She was taken anonymously by E. A. Reeves, former Map Curator and Instructor in Surveying to the Royal Geographical Society. Reeves, a friend of many explorers, knew Fawcett very well, for he was one of his first students at the Society. Just before Fawcett started on his last journey, he came with his son to see Reeves and say "Good-bye". They had often discussed psychic matters, and Fawcett had related many of his occult experiences.

Although Mrs Fawcett was not introduced by name, Red Cloud revealed that he knew who she was by addressing her as "little Fawcett lady". He told her that her son had died, but that her husband was then still alive. "He is an advanced psychic," said the guide. Mrs Fawcett understood the reference, for her husband had made a great study of occultism in India and in Ceylon. He was known to be a mystic by many of his friends.

"It was your husband that Rattin found," said Red Cloud, "but it is no use anyone going out to look for him. It would only be a waste of time and money. The knowledge your husband has gained is astonishing. Men would give kingdoms to have it."

At subsequent séances, Reeves received spirit messages from Fawcett, not only through Estelle Roberts, but through two other mediums. These clearly established that Fawcett had died in 1935. When Reeves told me this fascinating story, I arranged to have a special séance so that I could talk to Red Cloud and learn from him what had happened to Fawcett during his years of silence.

"I have been talking to Fawcett in my world," said Red Cloud. Then the guide repeated what he had told Mrs Fawcett when she came for a sitting: "I said to her that her husband was in the jungle living amongst the people. He travelled up-country, inland, after sending her a necklet, which she had placed in a museum.

"For a number of years he dwelled with the tribe, who looked upon him as their king, a gentle, loving soul whom they worshipped. They endeavoured to learn 'the white man's magic', as they called it. He lived more or less as a prisoner with them and found it difficult to get away. He endeavoured to become reconciled and to learn the magic which they knew and practised. Thus he sent many mental messages to his wife and to others whom he contacted."

This was a reference to Fawcett's occult powers, for several people had spoken of receiving telepathic messages from the explorer. Red Cloud referred to Fawcett's sufferings: "He had various bouts of fever caused by the humid and dense atmosphere in the jungle, the habits of the people and the insects. Although he recovered once or twice from the fever, it left its mark on his body. It was this fever that caused his passing into my world. Fawcett's frame had become emaciated owing to the difficulties and privations he had experienced."

Chapter 6
SÉANCE ANSWER TO PRAYER

MY most moving experience in the Estelle Roberts séance room came when I was addressed by an unknown spirit communicator. About half-way through one sitting, Red. Cloud said to me, almost casually: "There is a girl here who has approached me to get into touch with her mother on earth. She will give her own evidence."

"Do I know her?" I asked.

"No," the guide replied, "but you can help her."

The trumpet slowly moved towards me and a voice, obviously belonging to a young girl, said: "I will. All right. I will..."

From long experience I knew that the way to get the best results was to encourage the communicators to speak, not to ply them with questions which could have a rebuffing effect. "Come along," I urged, "you are going to try to give me a message. Come and talk to me."

The voice replied: "I will if I am allowed to talk. A kind man brought me here."

Then, very slowly, but distinctly, she declared: "My name is Bessy Manning. I died with tuberculosis last Easter. I have brought my brother, Tommy, with me; he was killed by a motor car. My mother has prayed because she reads your paper, and has asked, that someday the great guide, Red. Cloud, would bring me here."

In the psychic journal which I edited at the time, I had described some of these voice séances, and Bessy was indicating that her mother had read what I had printed. "I will send a message to your mother tomorrow," I told the girl.

Bessy expressed gratitude and continued: "Tell Mother that I still have my two long plaits. I am twenty-two, and I have got blue eyes. Tell her I want her to come here. Could you bring her?" Very wistfully she added, "She is not rich—she is poor."

"I will see if I can bring her," I replied.

"She is so unhappy," Bessy went on. "She says she lost both of us. You will help her, won't you? God will bless you if you help her. Thank you . . . thank you . . . thank you. . . ."

"Before I can send a message to your mother," I told Bessy, "I must know where she lives, for I do not know her."

Bessy's reply came without hesitation. "I will tell you," she said. Slowly and distinctly she gave the address, "14, Canterbury Street, Blackburn".

"Red Cloud," I said, "there must be thousands who pray for comfort, like her mother."

"I have only one instrument," he answered, with a note of sadness in his voice.

"Will you invite her mother to the next séance?" I asked. "Will I?" he replied. "Would you?"

I had never heard of Bessy Manning. I did not know whether there was a Mrs Manning, or whether there was a Canterbury Street in Blackburn, but my confidence, built on years of experience with Red Cloud, was such that I knew the spirit information was correct.

On the following morning, without the slightest doubt in my mind, I sent this telegram to Mrs Manning at 14, Canterbury Street, Blackburn: "Your daughter, Bessy, spoke to us at Red Cloud's circle last night." I received no reply, so I telegraphed again. Two days later, on the Monday, there were two letters from Mrs Manning.

The first one read: "I don't know whom I have to thank for the great joy you have given me. I thank you with all my heart and soul for the telegram I received last Saturday. I wanted to shout it from the house-tops. I laughed and cried all at once. What a wonderful spirit Red Cloud is, and how good and kind you all are! I feel sure you will carry your kindness further and let me know what my Bessy said.

"Oh, the glorious happiness to me and mine In my next letter I shall defray the cost of the telegram. Please don't be offended. It is only fair. How can I ever thank you enough? That bit of paper is more to me than untold gold. I will pray with all my heart for all of you, and especially for Mrs Roberts. You will tell me, won't you, if she sent me a little message. It is a wonderful, glorious truth, and again I thank you so much. Also my husband and my other two daughters thank you."

In her other letter Mrs Manning wrote: "I have received your second telegram. I am sorry to have caused you to have to send a second one, and I am so thankful for your wonderful kindness. You must not have received my letter which I posted on Sunday. I was very upset not being able to send you a return telegram, as things are not very bright at present. I want you to understand how grateful we all are. We would do anything possible to repay your great goodness. You don't know what it means to us.

"My daughter passed on last Easter Monday, and my son was killed nearly nine years ago. Had it not been for getting in touch with a Spiritualist family, I would have been raving mad. I am longing to know what Bessy said. I want to comfort others as I have been. We don't get real good mediums here. It must be great to hear Mrs Estelle Roberts and the other great ones. I wish I had the glorious gift. Again, I thank you so very much."

I regard Bessy Manning's return as flawless evidence for the afterlife. No theories of telepathy or the subconscious mind can explain it away. No suggestion of collusion or any other kind of fraud can be entertained. Mrs Manning had never met Estelle Roberts, or corresponded with her or any member of her family. Neither had she written to me or anyone who attended these voice séances. Yet her daughter's full name and address had been given, accompanied by a complete message which was accurate in every detail.

Later, when I met Mrs Manning, she told me that she had prayed night and day for evidence that her daughter lived beyond the grave. Her prayer had been heard and answered. How a prayer uttered in Blackburn can produce a response in Middlesex, I do not know. All that I do know is that it happened. This séance communication proves that some requests are heard, and that there is an organisation in the Beyond able to provide the answer when conditions are appropriate.

I arranged for Mrs Manning to come to London for the next voice séance. Her husband was unemployed. It was obviously a time of difficulty for her. I met her at St Pancras Station on, this, her first visit to London. She was full of excitement as I showed her some of the sights of the city before driving her down to Teddington, where the voice séances were held.

It was not long before Bessy, speaking through the

trumpet, addressed her overjoyed mother. "Ma," she said excitedly, "it's Bessy speaking."

"Yes, Bessy," replied her mother.

Her daughter was so full of excitement that halfway through her conversation the trumpet dropped, a sure sign that she could not hold the "power".

"Bessy," her mother said, "this is wonderful. You know how your mother loves you, don't you?"

"It is wonderful," Bessy replied. "God bless you, Ma. Tell Father not to worry. Tommy is here, too," she added. "We are here together. Tommy is also anxious to speak to you, Ma. It is so wonderful I don't know how to talk.... I am so excited."

The Lancashire dialect was obvious in the mother's voice when she answered: "Don't get excited, love. Talk to Mother. Do you come into the home, Bessy?"

"You know I do," she replied. "I try to talk to you there. Day after day you talk to my picture. You stand in front of it, you pick it up and kiss it, and I watch you all the time."

Later, Mrs Manning assured me that this was true. Often, in her grief, she would take her daughter's photograph, kiss it and talk to it. Bessy, to show that she knew what was happening in her own home, said to her mother: "You were telling Father about his boots this morning, weren't you, Ma?,,

"That is quite right," replied Mrs Manning.

"You said they wanted mending, didn't you, Ma?"

"I understand what you mean, Bessy," was the answer.

"My Ma, I called her Ma," said Bessy. In repeating Bessy's words to enable the stenographer to record them verbatim, I thought that Bessy once said "Mother". She instantly corrected me by saying "Ma", which was her usual greeting for her mother.

More evidence followed as Bessy referred to the beads that her mother was wearing, saying that these were once her property, and that she had worn them before she died. This, I later learned, was accurate.

"It was a big shock for you when Tommy was killed," were Bessy's last words to her mother. Red Cloud followed and said, "She brought the boy, Tommy, with her." Then, as he so often did, he slipped another item of evidence into his next sentence: "Tommy is named after his father."

When the séance was over, Mrs Manning was weeping, but they were tears of joy, not sorrow. "I am the happiest woman in the world," she said.

The following morning, before she returned to Blackburn, Estelle Roberts gave Mrs Manning a private sitting at which, I later learned, Bessy continued to prove her identity with detail after detail, none of which the medium could have known. She sent messages to other members of the family, and one to her fiancé. "Tell Billy," she said, "that I still remember the ring he sent me—the one I wore when I was buried."

A few days later, Mrs Manning sent me this letter, doubtless so that I could have her own testimony:

"I am writing this for the comfort of others, knowing I shall be ridiculed by some, laughed at by a few, but blessed by many. My only son, whom I adored, was killed by a motor. He was a dear little chap, who loved me very dearly. I was frantic—utterly crushed. I lost all hope. All my ambitions lay buried in his grave.

"Eight years later, my daughter Bessy passed on, one of

the most lovable and sweetest girls who ever lived. Just before the end, she said, 'If it is possible at all, I will come back.' I knew she would keep that promise. She has come in the most unexpected manner. I had often heard of the Red Cloud circle.

"It came as a big surprise to me to receive a telegram from Mr Barbanell telling me my daughter had come through, asking for her mother and telling them where she lived. I was astonished and overjoyed at the news. Through his kindness it was made possible for me to go to London and attend the circle. It was a great experience. Everywhere I was met with kindness. I heard many spirit voices and all were recognised. It was most amazing.

"I heard my own daughter speak to me, in the same old loving way, and with the self-same peculiarities of speech. She spoke of incidents that I know for a positive fact no other person could know. I, her mother, am the best judge, and I swear before Almighty God it was Bessy. She told me she had brought her brother with her, told of him being killed and gave his name. She spoke of many things that have passed in our home, things that were far from my mind at the time.

"I thank God, with all my heart and soul. He answered my prayers, and I have prayed, long and often. I have no fear of so-called death. I am looking forward to the glorious meeting with my loved ones."

The years went by, and I forgot about Bessy and her mother. The war had intervened, and there was so much to do. Estelle Roberts decided to renew her voice séances in the new home to which she had moved. I was delighted to find that her mediumship was as powerful as ever, and the results equally as impressive.

At one of them, Red Cloud said to me: "I have a visitor for you. Hold on." Through the trumpet, smeared as usual with its luminous paint, I heard the word "Hello" uttered three times. As this seemed to be a communicator making the first effort, I spoke words of encouragement. The woman's tones that came through the trumpet said: "I know that voice. You helped me very much by enabling me to talk to my daughter."

Quick as a flash, before she gave her name, I guessed it was Mrs Manning speaking, though I had not heard of her passing. She had returned to complete the story, to say "that the glorious meeting with my loved ones" which she had anticipated was now a reality. "I have got Bessy and Tommy here," she said through the trumpet. "Can you tell my family? Just give them my love and tell them I am helping. My dear ones would like to know."

I sent a copy of this spirit message to the old Blackburn address, but my letter came back with the envelope marked "Gone away". I was disappointed that Mrs Manning's family could not have the mother's message. Then, to my surprise, I received a letter from another address in Blackburn. It was written by a Mrs J. Smith, who described herself as a daughter of Mrs Manning. Someone had seen a printed reference I had made to her mother's return and had sent Mrs Smith a copy of it.

"I am her youngest daughter," she wrote. "My sister and I are the only remaining family on this earth. I can't tell you the joy and gladness the message gave me. I felt I wanted to run out and tell the world. Instead of which I sat down and cried. I felt humble and ashamed that I had begun to doubt and despair that I would ever hear of that beloved person again."

Her mother, she added, had suddenly died without the chance to say farewell. She was alone when she had a seizure. By the time the daughters reached her side, it was too late for their mother to speak.

"It was a cruel blow, for, with her passing, the sunshine of life went," wrote Mrs Smith. Years had dragged on and she was beginning to despair. Now she had received the answer to her prayers. "It is the grandest thing that can ever happen to me," was her summing-up.

Chapter 7
DISCERNING OF SPIRITS

JUDGING from the Bible, clairvoyance and other forms of mediumship were part of the normal practices of the early Christian Church. When you read Chapter XII of the First Epistle to the Corinthians you find that St Paul enumerates the "spiritual gifts" concerning which "I would not have you ignorant". His listing of these gifts is a good summary of modern forms of mediumship. He describes clairvoyance as the "discerning of spirits".

Every Sunday night, a quarter of a million people in Britain, according to my estimate, witness demonstrations of "discerning of spirits", the most common psychic gift, at one of the four thousand Spiritualist services that are held. No lights are lowered for these demonstrations. The medium singles out members of the congregation, describes spirit forms that she can see with them and relays the communicators' messages.

The acid test of the clairvoyance is that it must be evidential. The description given by the medium must so fit the communicator that it brings recognition to the recipient. The messages must be characteristic and succeed in establishing the identity of the transmitter.

Any suggestion that the medium is conveying what she receives telepathically from her hearers does not fit all the facts. Telepathy is a rare and almost freakish happening. Clairvoyance is so common that there are at least four thousand mediums regularly demonstrating it every Sunday. It would be a very difficult task for a medium to "tune in" telepathically to the one person in a crowded audience whose mind she wanted to fathom. Most of her listeners hope to receive a spirit message from the medium. These accumulated mental desires would present a barrier of conflicting thoughts.

I witnessed an impressive demonstration in this connection. The medium, Joseph Benjamin, was giving clairvoyance at a large public meeting at which there were many strangers. He pointed to one woman and said, referring to the successful messages he had already given: "You are wondering whether I get all this out of their minds. I will show you the difference between telepathy and clairvoyance. This is what is in your mind," he told the woman, and proceeded to relate the problems which she admitted were troubling her.

"Now this is not in your mind," he added, "because it comes from your dead father, and he says you will have to make inquiries to prove that he is right." There followed a message for the recipient to verify with her mother. Even in this case, however, it does not prove that the medium was obtaining the first part of his communication telepathically. It is conceivable that he received the information from his guide.

The sceptic might argue that what is regarded as clairvoyance is trickery, and refer to "mind-readers" on the stage who baffle audiences with the accuracy of their replies. The vaudeville "mind-reader" uses a code and frequently employs accomplices. The bandage over his assistant's eyes is either transparent or so arranged that it can be seen through, partially or wholly.

No "mind-reader" could transmit, week after week and year after year, before a different audience every Sunday night, and often on week nights, messages that the recipients say they recognise as emanating from people no longer on earth. Mediums who demonstrate clairvoyance regularly at Spiritualist services would not last very long if, wherever they went, they gave the same messages to the same accomplices. Sooner or later, and I think sooner, they would be found out. The amount of blackmail or "hush money" that would have to be paid to confederates would be far more than the clairvoyants obtain for their services. Their usual fee in most cases does not exceed a guinea. I know every worthwhile medium and have no hesitation in saying that at the best they earn only a modest living.

The spirit forms seen by clairvoyants look solid, real and natural, just like the rest of humanity. They are not transparent wraiths or ghostly spectres. These belong to the realm of fiction rather than to fact. Benjamin, when I asked him, said he had never once seen the conventional ghost, but in over twenty years of mediumship he has seen and described thousands of spirit beings who presented themselves to his vision.

It has always been a source of satisfaction that I knew one of Britain's greatest exponents of clairvoyance, Tom Tyrell, a Blackburn medium. His demonstrations were so extraordinary that when I heard him the first time I doubted their genuineness. They seemed too good to be true. He specialised in reciting the details conveyed on memorial cards. Thus his clairvoyance would include the full name of the communicator, the address where he had lived on earth—this was complete even to the number or name of the house, the street or road, the district and town—the age of the individual when he died, and the date of death.

Tyrell told me that when he began to develop his clairvoyance he was determined to make it as perfect as possible. Tyrell made a pact with his guide. The medium said he would not transmit any spirit messages unless the communicator held in his hand a replica of his memorial card, which Tom would read.

Having by this means established, without any possible doubt, the communicator's identity, Tom was then ready to convey the message. Unusual names thus presented no difficulty to the medium, although they sometimes intrigued him. Once, at Birmingham, in a large public meeting when I was present, Tyrell paused in the midst of reading a memorial card because the address puzzled him. "Is there a Rotten Park Road in this city?" he asked. "Yes," he was assured.

What do mediums hear and see when they practise "discerning of spirits"? For many years, Estelle Roberts has been rightly regarded as one of the most brilliant demonstrators of this form of public mediumship. Her psychic vision, she says, may be subjective or objective. When it comes within the first category, she sees spirit forms even though her eyes are closed. It is a mental, or inner, process in which she seems to be using a kind of "psychic eye". When her vision is objective, the spirit forms appear to be as real and solid as people on earth.

Her gift of clairaudience functions simultaneously. She "hears" the voices of the spirit communicators, who seem to be addressing her. When they are close enough, she is able to watch the movements of their lips. Their speech appears to have a softer tone than mortal voices.

With public clairvoyance, she penetrates another dimension of being. In the distance she sees the dead individuals who are waiting to establish their identity. Through the years, Estelle Roberts says she has noticed that unfortunately there are always many more spirit forms than she can possibly describe in the time at her disposal. At first, they stand grouped together, not necessarily close to those in the" audience with whom they are associated and whom they hope to reach.

They realise that they cannot succeed in making their presence known without the permission and help of the medium's guide. When a would-be communicator is singled out by the guide, the individual leaves the group and moves to the vicinity of the relative or friend in the audience whom he or she desires to reach. This action also indicates to the medium which person in the audience is to be addressed. Once this fact has been established, the spirit form returns to the platform and stands close to the medium so that she can obtain a clearer view. At the same time, she tunes in her clairaudience to hear what the spirit figure says.

Meanwhile, surrounding her on the platform, are Red Cloud and his band of helpers. Their function is to aid the communicators, to calm them if they are excited or overwrought, and to help them reproduce, for the purpose of recognition, their physical appearance and even their earthly clothing. When Estelle Roberts describes some physical infirmity that the communicator possessed on earth, it does not mean that this defect continues in, the afterlife. The earthly condition, as well as all other former characteristics, has to be temporarily duplicated to ensure recognition.

Once the identity has been fully established, these defects

fall away, and the medium sees the present spiritual status and appearance of the individual. Estelle Roberts has frequently noticed that people who have progressed in the spirit world are increasingly reluctant to reproduce their earthly characteristics. When the recipient has recognised the communicator, there is so rapid a transformation to his true spiritual status that the medium sometimes can hardly recognise that it is the same person.

In our world appearances are often deceptive. It is not always possible to be accurate in our judgment of someone's age. When the communicators show themselves to the medium, she has to assess the age at which they died by their spiritual appearance. There may be a similar margin of error in her judgment as in ours when we attempt to guess ages.

The time that has elapsed since death has also to be calculated by the medium, who bases her opinion on the communicator's aura or radiation. The more evolved they are, the more brilliant is the radiation emanating from them. There are occasions when this light is so dazzling that it obscures the features and even the distinguishing characteristics of sex. This is often the case with a child who has been in the Beyond for many years.

In addition to Red Cloud's band of helpers, there are watching a number of guides associated with those who wish to reveal their presence at the meeting. These experienced helpers form a protective circle round the medium. This prevents any impulsive spirit entity from pressing forward and interfering, even unconsciously, with the delicate vibrations necessary for messages to be accurately transmitted. Estelle Roberts told me: "The spirit communicators are drawn into this circle and isolated from the others while they give their messages. Even with all this elaborate precaution it is impossible to silence the shouts of those who surround the circle clamouring for recognition."

From the moment the medium walks on to the platform and until she is ready to give her demonstration, many of these dead individuals strive to attract her attention. She is, however, far too experienced to act upon their requests unless Red Cloud singles them out to communicate. Nevertheless, if she sees that one of them is in obvious distress, she mentally asks that this individual be given a chance to manifest. This clamour for recognition is pathetic, but sometimes it takes a humorous form. Once, in the babel of voices, she heard a shout above the din: "Hi, Mrs, give me a chance 1 The others have had a go." Death obviously had not transformed the Cockney dialect into the accents of an Oxford don. And why should it?

Red Cloud insists that each communicator must prove his own identity. He and his band will help, but, except on rare occasions, they will not give the evidence vicariously. Even when groups of relatives return together, each must present his or her own proofs of identity. Sometimes, when Estelle Roberts is doubtful about the authenticity of a spirit message, she will obtain confirmation from Red Cloud, who knows immediately whether the communicator is being truthful or otherwise. To one of his experience and knowledge the communicator's aura reveals all the owner's secrets, which makes deception impossible.

The act of death does not immediately change an individual's outlook or character. The medium assured me: "I sometimes see dead individuals who do not believe it is the will of God that communication should take place between this world and the next. I get dead people of all kinds of denominations coming to me and telling me I am doing wrong. Not content with that, they try to stop others from communicating."

She added that there were heartrending scenes when communicators realised they were not meeting with success. But the joy they experienced when they triumphed showed that they considered it well worth the effort.

Another brilliant medium who has recorded for me her sensations when demonstrating clairvoyance is Helen Hughes. Mackenzie King, when he was Prime Minister of Canada, always made a point of having a private séance with her whenever he visited Britain.

Her public displays of clairvoyance are always given at great speed and almost without pause. Frequently she breaks off in the middle of one spirit message to start another from a communicator who has suddenly made himself visible or audible to her. Knowing that the previous recipient will be disappointed at the thought that the message will not be completed, she provides reassurance by saying that she will return to it when she has successfully transmitted the new communication.

All her vitality and energy are poured into a demonstration that usually lasts about half an hour. Then she announces that the "power is waning" and she has to stop, otherwise the pull or drag is more than she can stand. It is significant that applause temporarily creates fresh power for stimulating the dwindling force. I have frequently noticed that when, at the end of her demonstration, the audience breaks into voluntary applause, she will stand up and successfully transmit one, or even two, more messages.

Even with years of experience, I am unable to say with exactitude what makes conditions good or bad for displays of mediumship in public or in private. Obviously vibrations have something to do with the results. At public meetings where hymns are sung and music played, the psychic demonstrations are inevitably better than at gatherings where there is neither music nor hymns.

The mental attitude of the audience, either individually or as a composite whole, also has a bearing on the results. Honest scepticism is no deterrent, but deliberate hostility and unwillingness to be receptive have a freezing effect on the medium, the communicator and the communication. Good humour and brightness of outlook are helpful. A dreary chairman or speaker will make the task harder for the clairvoyant who has to follow. An eloquent speaker who breaks the ice and stirs the audience makes the medium's task the lighter.

There is something in the voice of the recipient which is indicative to the medium. At the beginning of the message more than one person may try to claim it. I have noticed how eagerly Helen Hughes will listen to the would-be recipients and eliminate one of them by saying: "It is not your voice I want." Sometimes the problem is solved for the medium by seeing what she describes as a psychic light travelling from the communicator to the recipient.

I have tested the accuracy of her psychic vision in many ways. Once, after a public meeting, I showed her a photograph and said, half-jokingly: "If you are a medium, tell me who it is." Without a moment's hesitation, she replied: "I have seen him today . . . on the platform . . . he is the young airman with the foreign name I tried to give." She was right.

It was a photograph of a Polish airman. I had obtained it a few hours previously from a woman who had received a detailed spirit message concerning him from the medium. Occasionally she will correct herself because she had obviously not quite heard what was said. Sometimes, though she possesses no histrionic ability, she is so transformed that she seems to become the communicator. She assumes their postures and repeats their mannerisms.

Though I have witnessed her demonstrations of clairvoyance so many times that I could be forgiven for regarding them as a matter of course, I am still surprised at this medium's ability to point to people seated in different parts of the hall and tell them that they are related to one another and detail their relationships. Sometimes they had deliberately separated so that no clue could be given to the medium. After all, it is a fairly safe guess to assume that people sitting next to one another are in some way connected.

I listened with fascination at one meeting when Helen Hughes singled out six people seated together in one row. Her clairvoyance included descriptions and messages from dead relatives of all the six people. What made the evidence outstanding, however, was the fact that in each case she pointed to the right person in the group to whom the communicator was related, and announced what the relationship was.

Sometimes, in a very large and crowded hall, the communicators will show themselves to Helen Hughes on the platform, give evidential details about themselves, but offer no indication where the persons they want to reach are seated. Once this tactic on the part of a spirit figure had a remarkable sequel. The scene was the Caird Hall, Dundee, which seats nearly three thousand people. It was a crowded meeting. Mrs Hughes, in the course of her demonstration which followed my address, gave a detailed description of a girl whose name, she said, was Edith Proctor. Before the medium could transmit the spirit message, a woman seated in the balcony said she knew Edith Proctor. As the medium narrated evidential details concerning the girl, the recipient volunteered that she understood every one of them. She also acknowledged the accuracy of the medium's statement that Edith's father was with her in the spirit world.

Helen Hughes hesitated for a few seconds and then pointed to another woman seated in the middle of the hall. "You know Edith Proctor, too," she said. "Yes," came the reply. After another pause, Helen told the second woman, "You are her mother." This relationship was confirmed. Again the medium paused, and then said: "I hope you won't be embarrassed if I ask you a question." The woman smiled, and Helen continued: "I get the word 'Black'. Does that mean anything to you?" "Yes," was the answer. One more pause and the medium finally said: "Are you now Mrs Black?" The woman admitted that she was. The medium added that the daughter sent her congratulations on the re-marriage.

Helen Hughes returned to the first person who had acknowledged the message, and said: "This girl comes back to you. You must have known her very well." The reply was, "Yes."

"Do you live outside Dundee?" Again confirmation came. "Well, this girl did not live very far from you." That statement produced the recipient's final "Yes".

I asked this medium to explain how her psychic gifts functioned in public. "In clairvoyance, I see a spirit form as naturally as if I were using my physical eyes," she said. "I feel as though I am there and yet not there. First, before I begin to demonstrate, I have to make myself completely impassive. I can tune in at any time. When I do so, I can see with my spirit eyes and hear with my spirit ears. It is almost like opening or closing a door. It is a power within myself which I can either open or close. It is something within me that does the seeing and the hearing, something like an inner eye and an inner ear."

I quoted the case of Mrs Caradoc Evans, the authoress who writes under the names of Oliver Sandys and Countess Barcynska, who told me that after her husband's death she heard him "speak" with what she called the "ears of my heart". Helen Hughes thought this a good metaphor. "Although I sometimes hear with my ears," she said, "mostly I 'hear' with my solar plexus. I am conscious of something which I can only call, for want of a better word, `power'. This `power' seems to energise, quicken and flood through me.

"I feel as if an electric force, which partakes of something magnetic in nature, is at my feet, and, rising, flows through me. When it is working well and is really strong, there seems to be something like a series of telegraph wires, a range of vibrations, along which come the messages. After a time, the 'power' dies down. I cannot pick up the vibrations easily, and then, as I am liable to become less accurate, I always have to stop. One must never force this strange `power', for fear of inaccuracy, and also because it imposes a strain on the system.

"I seem to work much on the methods of the radio. I have also what I can only describe as a little 'television' set inside me, because I can see and describe scenes that have happened in the past, or which may be going to happen in the future. I actually hear the spirit voices sometimes speaking in my ear. At other times I hear them in the region of my solar plexus. The voices vary in clarity, some being as loud as ordinary physical voices and others whisperings or muffled tones."

When they speak in her ears, and this is the most usual way of hearing, Helen Hughes can gauge the height of the speaker by the direction of the voice.

The recipients of spirit messages play an important part. If they speak up loudly that creates a vibration which assists the medium. It also encourages the spirit communicator, who can hear the voice of the person he is trying to reach.

I asked her about the problem of when two or three people claim to recognise a clairvoyant description. Usually, she said, a spirit light comes from the communicator and moves to the person for whom the message is intended. When the light does not appear, the medium knows which is the right recipient because when she hears the response for whom it is intended something "clicks" within her. This "click", she said, was caused by the excitement of the spirit communicator at obtaining recognition.

She explained the fact that she breaks off one message to start another by saying that the voices, butting in with rapidity, often do not give her much time—evidence of their owners' anxiety to reach loved ones. Sometimes one spirit speaker will try to use the vibration created by the previous communicator. When a spirit voice fails to make itself heard, her guide has to step in, but that is never as effective as direct communication. Her guide has explained to me that it is easier when those who desire to communicate use their own wavelengths. Sometimes, however, they become too excited and so he has to speak on their behalf.

"When I give clairvoyance," said Helen Hughes, "I see a spirit form as naturally as if I were using the physical eye. I am not aware of any abnormal sensation until I begin to respond to the feelings or characteristics of the communicator who appears to me. These sensations may be of happiness or sorrow, anxiety or peace. Sometimes I find myself responding to the last sensations the spirit speaker experienced before leaving the physical body. It appears that by coming into contact with the earth atmosphere again there is an association of the old ideas and impressions, causing the last earth experience of the spirit speaker to recur temporarily."

Her mediumship often functions spontaneously in the street, on trains and elsewhere. Because these spirit entities can see her, they frequently greet her. Usually this takes place in the morning rather than in the evening. "The freshness of the morning somehow makes them clearer to my vision," she said.

Frequently in railway carriages Helen Hughes has been faced with the problem of eager spirit communicators who show themselves clearly, converse with her, and then ask for messages to be given to one of the occupants of the compartment. To break down the traditional British reserve and talk with a fellow-passenger in a train is bad enough, but to pass on a spirit message to a complete stranger is to risk a rebuff. Occasionally she has taken a chance. When she has transmitted the message it is almost invariably received with gratitude.

Newcomers who expect spirit return to be a solemn happening are surprised to find that public clairvoyance is very human, a mixture of seriousness and humour, a recital of occurrences that sometimes appear trivial but are highly evidential to the receivers of the messages. As I have already explained, the whole process is governed by vibrations which make for success when they are vibrant, and fail when they are tense or sluggish. Humour, which speedily breaks down any rigidity, is conducive to better results. I have in front of me detailed notes I made of a demonstration, lasting for an hour and a half, given by Joseph Benjamin. The medium said to one woman that he could see with her a girl who had died of consumption and who was making her first return. Benjamin gave the girl's name, told how she had died—choking with consumption—and added these extraordinary details: "She lived near you, on the other side of the road, on the corner, in the upstairs part of a house." All this brought eager nods of assent.

Then the medium's voice rose—a note of excitement always creeps in when he effects close touch with the communicator—as he added: "This girl had four fingers, not five." "Yes," exclaimed the surprised woman, "she tried to hide the fact."

This is a good example of what I mean by evidence. It is not everyone who has a missing finger. Its absence helped to clinch the owner's identity.

An indication of how information is conveyed to the medium came in the course of his next message, when, after transmitting some proofs, he asked the young woman: "Why do I see 'New Zealand' written over your head?" She replied, "I have just arrived from New Zealand."

A very human touch came in a succeeding message, prefaced by the medium asking a woman: "Can I be 'frank?" When she gave her assent, he relayed this surprising spirit communication: "Thank God you divorced my grandson!" The audience was fascinated by the detailed nature of some of these messages. This was seen in the next communication from a man who must have been a character. After giving his name, Springer, and saying that he had died quickly because of a heart attack, Benjamin added that this man had sold fruit, had two sons, was known as "Old Barney", but sometimes familiarly called "Old Barney". It is not surprising that with this wealth of detail the woman who received the message had no difficulty in recognising Springer.

She quickly agreed when the communicator recalled how she had bought some fruit from him, and he had refused her money because at the time he thought she needed it more than he did. Finally, the clairvoyant rounded off his message by telling the woman: "You are lucky to have your leg, because the hospital wanted to amputate it!"

To a grey-haired woman, Benjamin narrated at length mysterious happenings in her home that involved the inexplicable falling of a picture and the equally strange behaviour of a musical jug. He knew of these occurrences, said Benjamin, because he was being told about them by the woman's dead husband, who said he was responsible, and it was his means of trying to attract her attention. This, of course, may sound trivial, but it showed that the husband was able to convey his knowledge of happenings in his wife's home.

Next, the medium pointed to a man seated by the woman,

and said: "That's your second husband—no, it's your third!" He was right. This led the man to praise his wife with: "If every woman were like her . . ." The clairvoyant speedily replied: "That's why her other husbands come back!"

Acknowledging the accuracy of another communication, the receiver inquired whether the clairvoyant could give any guidance on a medical verdict that had proved worrying. Benjamin, suggesting this might be a case where spirit healing could help, pointed out that the doctors were not infallible in their diagnoses. "A doctor told me that I had six months to live," he said. "Six months later, the doctor had died."

"How does a man like Benjamin discover his mediumistic talents?" you might ask. In his teens he heard about Spiritualist meetings in a neighbouring street. He went with some friends, their idea being that it might be fun to create a disturbance. There was no heckling, for the visiting medium singled him out with a highly evidential spirit message from a cousin which sent the youthful Benjamin home in a daze. His curiosity aroused, he returned the following week. This time, as he sat in the audience, he fell into what he thought was a sleep, but it was his first experience of the trance state.

"When I came to," he said, "the whole crowd was standing round me. One man volunteered that I had given him a wonderful message from his dead father." After that it was only a question of time. As his psychic powers developed he was bombarded with requests for séances. His work as a tailor's presser involved a thirteen-hour day and meant that he could never start to function as a medium before about 10 p.m. A decision to make mediumship his whole-time service was inevitable.

What is his reward? It is very modest, despite the fact that he is among the most successful public clairvoyants today. The society that organises his twice-weekly public meetings expects to cover the expenses involved by making a charge of a shilling for admission, but this is waived for old-age pensioners. Both halls seat about one hundred and fifty people. For his private séances, which have to be limited because psychic power cannot be turned on like a tap, the fee is a guinea. There is no fortune in mediumship.

Chapter 8
WHEN A MEDIUM IS ENTRANCED

WHAT happens when a medium enters the trance state and willingly surrenders control of her body to a spirit guide? The action is always a voluntary one, for the essence of mediumship is that the medium is the mistress of her own physical being. It speaks volumes for the trust and respect that mediums have for their guides that they consent to this willing act of surrender, which they know will not be abused. It is difficult for outsiders to appreciate the love and affection that bind guide and medium. Through the years, the human instrument receives evidence of sustenance and help from the spirit guide, who is invisible to others but is a daily, living reality to her.

I asked Helen Hughes to describe her reactions as she went into trance and came out of it. The process is akin to falling asleep, she said. As a preparation, she relaxes physically and mentally; she becomes aware of a gradual drugging of her consciousness which reminds her of the sensations accompanying the inhalation of chloroform.

Coming out of the trance state is similar to awakening from sleep. If the trance condition has been deep and prolonged, she returns to normality with the feeling of having travelled from some distant place. This sensation of travelling is more in evidence after her guides, as distinct from other spirit entities, have taken possession.

She always emerges from the trance state feeling much better than before it. It brings her a feeling of renewal, which she compares with a glass of water being emptied and then refilled with fresh water. She described the trance experience as quite pleasant. It is preceded by a welcome feeling of complete relaxation and resignation. The after effects are similar to those which follow a healthy sleep. Her considered opinion is that the practice of trance mediumship cannot have any deleterious effect on the health, provided, of course, that it is done in moderation.

Sometimes her guides allow others to take temporary control. When this happens, the medium's voice, gestures and bodily pose alter, and assume the characteristics of the communicator.

I have had very many séances with Helen Hughes, the most outstanding, from the evidential viewpoint, being those which have taken place impromptu, when she has yielded to the trance condition because of her psychic awareness that some worthwhile information is to be transmitted.

There are three regular communicators. The first is White Feather, her Indian guide, a figure of dignity, with slow and deliberate speech. "He is the philosopher, the teacher and the comforter," says the medium, "and the great moulding influence in my life." Then there is Granny Anderson, a North-country woman with the distinctive dialect and idioms of that area, with a homely humour and outspoken manner. Lastly, there is Mazeeta, a disarming Indian child.

If you heard the voices of these three guides coming from a radio set you would find it impossible to believe that they emanated only from one person. Were it all done by superb acting, Helen Hughes would find it more lucrative to portray character impersonations as a means of livelihood. Sometimes at these trance séances you have a succession of communicators, with the three guides speaking at the beginning, and two of them returning at the end. Granny contents herself with one communication, but what she says is very much to the point.

The word "trance" as applied to mediumship is really a misnomer. The number of mediums who are completely unconscious while under spirit control is comparatively small. There are degrees of "trance" mediumship ranging from the elementary stages, which are really examples of overshadowing, to complete insensibility. In some of the lighter forms, the medium is aware of what is being said through her lips but has no control over the communication.

Many mediums have described their sensations while being controlled. Some say that they listen to the communication coming through them, but they seem to be standing some distance away from themselves. Others assert that while they, too, hear what is being said, they appear to be occupying a position above themselves. A few are conscious of experiencing "out-of-the-body" travels and are able to narrate what they have seen and heard in distant places.

My mature judgment is that even when the trance reaches the stage of complete oblivion, this does not mean that the medium's subconscious mind has been entirely eliminated. I would assert that it is very rare, in any form of mediumship, to receive a hundred per cent. of spirit communication. All control, which is a form of possession, is achieved through the medium's subconscious mind. The degree of success depends upon the spirit mastery that is attained.

Though many attempts have been made to invent mechanical contrivances, none has worked without the presence of a medium. Even with the finest invention—some of these, including the receipt of spirit messages through a sealed

Morse instrument, I will describe later—the medium had to be present to supply the necessary power to make the appliance work.

Sir Ernest Fisk, one of the greatest radio experts, who was associated with Marconi in his first experiments in this direction, expressed his conviction to me that mechanical spirit communication was possible. If the necessary funds were available, he said, to finance the research required, he was convinced that an apparatus could be devised. In his view, it was only a question of being able to register radiations from the spirit world. Whether such an achievement is possible I cannot say. Whether it would be desirable is highly controversial. At humanity's comparatively low present evolution I shudder to think what would be the result if millions of people could flick a knob and receive spirit communications, in much the same way that they can see television or listen to the radio.

Meanwhile, we are dependent on human instruments. It is obvious that the messages must be affected to some degree by the mentalities through which they are transmitted. Mediums are not telephones or television sets. They are human beings with ideas, opinions, prejudices and preconceptions of their own. To some extent these must colour the results. Allowance must always be made for the proportion, large or small, that can be the result of the medium's own subconscious thinking. This is an elementary precaution, dictated by common sense.

Most people do not realise how many of their actions are controlled by their subconscious minds. When we were babies, the process of learning to walk required a determined, concentrated effort. Years of habit have made walking almost a mechanical process. Now our mind flashes a message to the subconscious that we are going to walk. Immediately, it sets in motion all the necessary muscles, nerves, sinews and movements of blood that are necessary to get the legs to walk. A similar activity is enacted in the case of talking and, indeed, for all bodily functions.

Before mediums are controlled, their mental acquiescence is the first stage in stilling their consciousness. The spirit communicator, in taking charge, has, in order to achieve any degree of entrancement, to subdue the medium's consciousness, and then become the directive intelligence by asserting mastery over the subconscious mind. It has for many years been a subject of controversy as to whether trance mediumship is improved by the medium having more or less culture and learning. One school argues that when the medium knows little, the degree of subconscious resistance is minimised. On the other hand, the argument runs, the more the mediums know, the better instruments they become.

My own view is that the more we know the less dogmatic do we become. Even after a hundred and twenty years of mediumship, its techniques are still subject to heated discussion. From my fairly lengthy experience I could furnish examples to confirm both schools of opinion. I recall an illuminating experience with one of our greatest mediums, whose guide made a certain pronouncement. Then he said: "That is not my view. It is an idea that is dominant in my medium's subconscious mind. The only way that I can continue to function in freedom is to express this dominant thought and get it out of the way."

Although many descriptions have been given of the

processes said to be employed in the production of psychic phenomena, they are never so precise as to enable us to achieve the results ourselves. We are all spiritual beings here and now. We possess, albeit in embryo, all the attributes of our spiritual nature that we will express after death. We will not become spiritual beings because we die. Therefore, anything that is achieved through mediumship by discarnate beings could be performed by us while we are on earth, if we knew how to do it.

It may be that one barrier is the fact that we are expressing ourselves in a different time-space relationship from that in which we will manifest after the body's dissolution. There are authenticated, though isolated, cases of a living man being able to control and speak through a trance medium, but the phenomenon was organised by a spirit guide who took the initiative in the matter.

The East is full of accounts of yogis and fakirs who are able, by extending their psychic powers, to achieve a mastery of mind over matter and perform astonishing feats. They reveal processes analogous to mediumship. I can foresee that if the secrets of mediumistic techniques were revealed in a fashion that enabled human beings to do what only spirit guides can perform in the séance room, it would lead to complete confusion. Thus it may be that complete knowledge is deliberately concealed. I have known investigators spend many years on psychic, experiments which they explained as having been achieved by a certain method. The sequel inevitably was that results came which could not have been produced by the theory propounded.

Chapter 9
SAVED FROM SUICIDE

A BRILLIANT man contemplated suicide because the death of his wife had left him inconsolable. You may not know his name but you will have heard of his achievement. I refer to Lionel Logue, the Australian voice specialist who cured King George VI of his stammering and became one of the monarch's most intimate friends. Their friendship ripened from the time when, as Duke of York, he first consulted Logue about his speech defect. The Australian became a regular and welcome visitor to Buckingham Palace, where he participated in the family gatherings. Whenever the King had to make an important speech, and especially a broadcast, Logue, at the Sovereign's request, was usually present, if only in the background.

Because he knew that Hannen Swaffer was a famous Spiritualist, Logue called on the journalist to enlist his aid in his cruel bereavement. Though he had reached the height of his professional career, Logue confessed that he found it hard to carry on now that his beloved wife was no longer by his side. He mourned her every hour of the day and was eager to know if he could possibly obtain proof of her survival. Swaffer promised to help. He approached Lilian Bailey and asked if she would come to his flat and give a sitting to "a man in great distress". The medium agreed and a date was arranged. "Naturally, I won't tell you anything about him," said Swaffer.

Mrs Bailey, like every other worthwhile medium, preferred

to know nothing about her sitters. Any knowledge of them, she has always found, acts as a deterrent. Besides, the less she knows, the more impressive is any evidence obtained through her mediumship. Swaffer introduced Lilian Bailey to Logue, but neither mentioned his name nor gave any hint as to his identity. "And so far as I know," said the journalist, "Logue's portrait had never appeared in newspapers."

Almost at the beginning of the séance, even before she entered her usual trance state, Mrs Bailey looked embarrassed because of a scene that had presented itself to her clairvoyant vision. "I don't know why it is," she said, "and I scarcely like to tell you, but King George V is here. He asks me to thank you for what you did for his son."

To the medium's surprise, Logue replied: "I quite understand." That was almost all that happened at the Australian's first séance. Lilian Bailey did add that she could see the spirit form of his wife. "But," said the medium, "she is too excited to do more than send her love to her husband."

Swaffer arranged for Logue to have a second sitting in his flat. He had to leave just before it began for a Guildhall banquet. Immediately he returned he was told how Mrs Logue had controlled the medium. A moving scene followed as the wife proved to her distracted husband that their love could bridge the gulf of death.

Logue was deeply overcome as his wife, to prove that she was familiar with what had happened since her passing, talked to him about the changes he had made in the house and garden which were unknown to anyone else present. That night, more and more evidence accumulated as Lilian Bailey's guide relayed intimate messages from Logue's partner in the Beyond. This guide, William Hedley Wootton, an officer who died in the First World War, is expert in transmitting evidence. One such item was the fact that Logue's pet name for his wife was "Muggsy". Wootton inquired: "Is there any question you want to ask?" Logue hesitated. Then he thought of an excellent question: "Does my wife want to say anything about the place where we first met?" Wootton, when he replied, said with a puzzled expression: "She is referring to a bird named Charlie. It is not a canary. It looks like a sparrow."

This answer overwhelmed Logue. Charlie Sparrow was his best friend. It was at Charlie's twenty-first birthday party that he had met the future Mrs Logue and fallen in love with her. Logue put his next question: "Does she remember the place?" The guide answered: "It was Free . . . Fremantle." Charlie Sparrow's house was in Fremantle. This evidence so impressed Logue that often at his subsequent meetings with Lilian Bailey he repeated it to her.

Next came a stern warning. His wife told him that he must not dream of taking his life because, instead of achieving the reunion he expected, it would only divide them. At that time the medium did not know that the thought of suicide was in Logue's mind. As a result of this séance, the speech specialist became very friendly with Mrs Bailey and her family. His wife continued, at successive sittings, to show detailed interest in all that concerned her husband. To indicate the closeness she maintained, I relate one incident.

When he moved from a large house to a flat, he asked at one séance if she could remember what had happened to the bed linen. Immediately came the answer that she wanted him to use the yellow sheets and pillowcases—this, you must agree, shows the wifely touch—and described the box where Logue later found them. These monthly sittings were held at first in the medium's Wembley home but afterwards, when he became ill, at his flat in Knightsbridge. The medium says that, of all the people she has met, she seldom knew of a husband and wife so devoted to each other.

It was Logue who volunteered to her that Spiritualism had enabled him to understand his work of correcting speech defects, which occupied the major part of his life. He realised, since he had received his séance proofs, that he had been guided to leave Australia, when there was no apparent reason, and to seek a new career in Britain. Without knowing why, at the time, he had sold up his home. There were no seeming prospects in England, and it appeared to be madness.

The medium is convinced that Logue was naturally psychic. This was borne out by the fact that often he knew instantly what was wrong with patients who consulted him, even before he made any diagnosis.

Having received his evidence of survival, Logue's life was transformed. Despair gave way to radiance brought by knowledge, a radiance that was evident when I met him. The last occasion was in a Spiritualist church. I was conducting the service of naming (Spiritualism's equivalent to christening) for Lilian Bailey's two grandsons. Logue, to show his gratitude to the medium for the comfort she had brought him, acted as godfather.

He told me that he made no secret of his Spiritualism. On several occasions he had described to King George VI his séances with Lilian Bailey, recounting the wonderful evidence he had received from his wife, and he had never met with hostility.

At one time, Logue was very concerned because one of his sons was dying. His wife, through Lilian Bailey, insisted that the boy would live. The verdict of all the eminent specialists that Logue had consulted was that his boy had no chance. His wife, however, proved to be right.

Eventually, Logue's illness ended with his passing. Lilian Bailey discovered that in his will he had bequeathed a royal chair to her. It was the one which had been specially brought from Windsor at the request of the King, when he was Duke of York, so that he could sit in it when he had his consultations with Logue. Because he had noticed her liking for this chair when she gave séances in his flat, Logue left it to the medium, when he went to meet his wife who had preceded him.

It was not long before the two of them returned at Lilian Bailey's home circle. When I asked her what Logue said, she replied that his happiness was indescribable. He had found spirit life was even more beautiful than he had hoped.

* * *

A hard-headed businessman, who took the most elaborate precautions to conceal his identity, was convinced of Spiritualism, through trance mediumship in thirty seconds. So painstaking were the safeguards he adopted to maintain his anonymity that he was known as the "Mystery Man". His story, as it unfolded itself, was a fascinating insight into human nature.

I had gone to Leeds to address a meeting of its Psychic Research Society at which Helen Hughes was to demonstrate clairvoyance. She asked me to join her at tea in a hotel, where, for the second time, she was meeting the "Mystery Man". Their previous meeting had been when he arrived for a séance.

His behaviour was extraordinary. When he came into the room, she asked him to take a seat. He did so, but said nothing. In fact, during the whole séance he never uttered one word. At the end of it, he left without breaking his silence. Afterwards, he showed her the copious notes he had made, but there was a blank where there was mentioned a name, district, or any reference that might give a clue to his identity.

At tea in the hotel, he was accompanied by two women. No introductions were made. All I could guess< from his conversation was that he seemed to be a typically shrewd, rugged Yorkshireman. You would have thought him as hard as nails. That night, however, at the public meeting, I saw another side of his nature. Helen Hughes gave one of the two women a spirit message that she said came from her son. As the medium added details that were obviously evidential, I noticed that tears rolled down the face of the Yorkshire-man, who, I assumed, was her husband.

Every word the medium said in connection with this son's message was recorded in shorthand by the other woman, who appeared to be a secretary. After the meeting, the Yorkshireman came to me, saying that he had observed I had taken notes. Could I let him have a transcript of the one message in which he was interested? "To save time," I said, "I will read my notes over to your companion." I did so. Our notes tallied.

When I came to the words "Doctor Bradley", which were part of the message given by Helen Hughes, the secretary involuntarily mentioned that this name was wrong. Her employer rebuked her for making this admission. The incident made me smile. Obviously, the Yorkshireman did not relish the idea of anybody piercing his elaborate veil of secrecy. That night, over supper, I recounted the incident to Helen Hughes.

The following morning she provided an unexpected sequel. She had been unable to sleep. While tossing restlessly in her bed, she heard the name "Bradbury". "That is the name I should have given, not Bradley," she said. The mistake was excusable to a clairaudient, who has to listen in. And the medium, very ill on that night, was not at her best.

It was all very well for Helen Hughes to obtain the correct name, but how was I to convey the information to the Yorkshireman? I printed an account of this happening, ending with the words, "Perhaps 'Mystery Man' will let me know if that is right." The day after my account was published in the psychic journal I edited, I received a telegram reading: "Mrs Hughes was quite right." It was signed "Mystery Man".

A fortnight later, "Mystery Man", still without disclosing his name, and of his own accord, sent me for publication the remarkable story of his psychic quest. He began with a reference to his nickname, and said he planned it that way, as only by remaining quite anonymous could any evidence offered to him be convincing. But now he felt it would be ungrateful and churlish not to make some public acknowledgement of "the saving grace vouchsafed to me through spiritual aid".

It was his son who had returned to him. The father described him as "Six feet one, and all muscle, as fine a specimen of an Englishman as it would be possible to meet." He was an all-round athlete, an excellent swimmer, oarsman and squash player. His army service was distinguished, as was his career. He took his medical degrees with medals and honours. Everything pointed to his becoming a fine surgeon. The father was unashamed in expressing the love that existed between them. They were tremendous pals, who went swimming, canoeing, motoring and shooting together, even attending the same gymnasium.

This, and the following sequence of seven photographs depict the whole process of materialising a spirit form. They were taken in about thirty minutes. An assistant holds the curtain to reveal the entranced medium Ethel Post-Parrish, of Pennsylvania, U.S.A.

A cloudy pillar of ectoplasm slowly builds from the medium to the height of a full-grown woman. Gradually the ectoplasm solidifies until finally the full figure emerges completely materialised. It is Silver Belle, an Indian girl said to be the medium's spirit guide.

104 THIS IS SPIRITUALISM

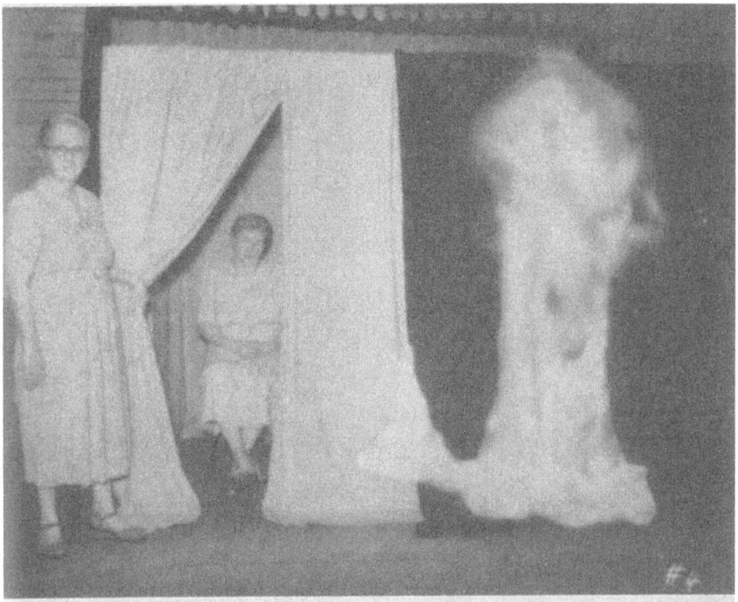

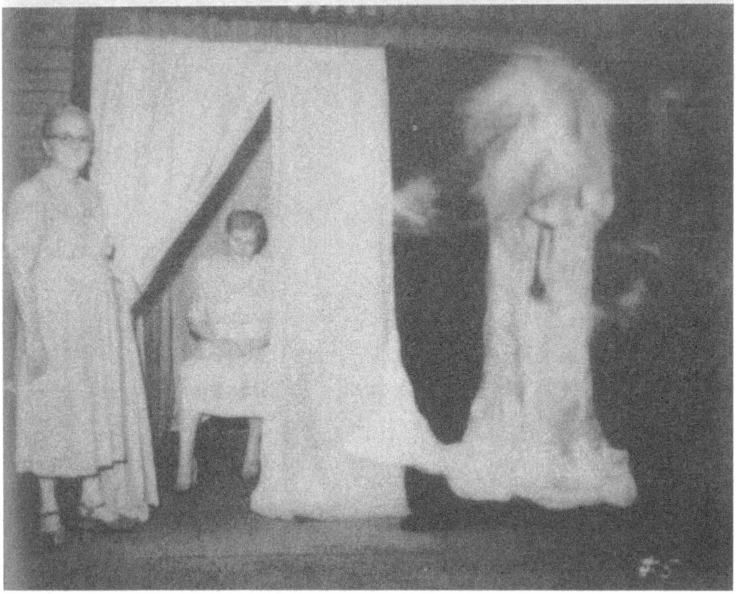

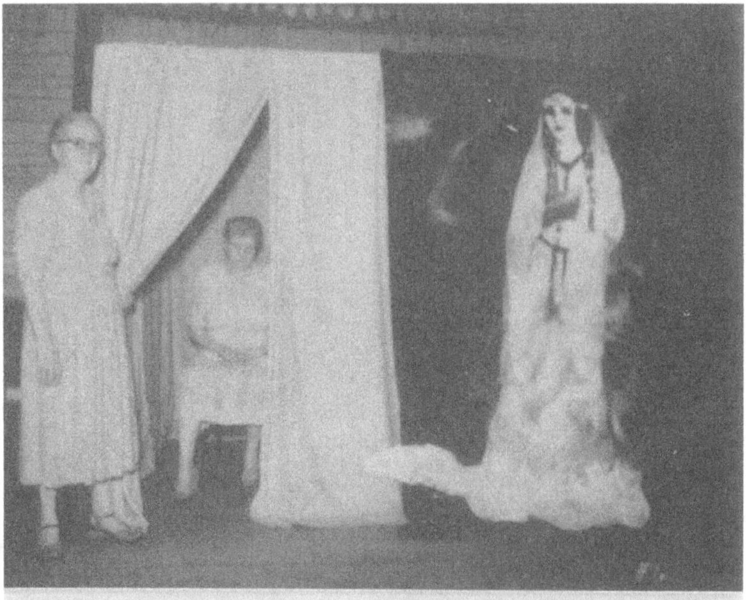

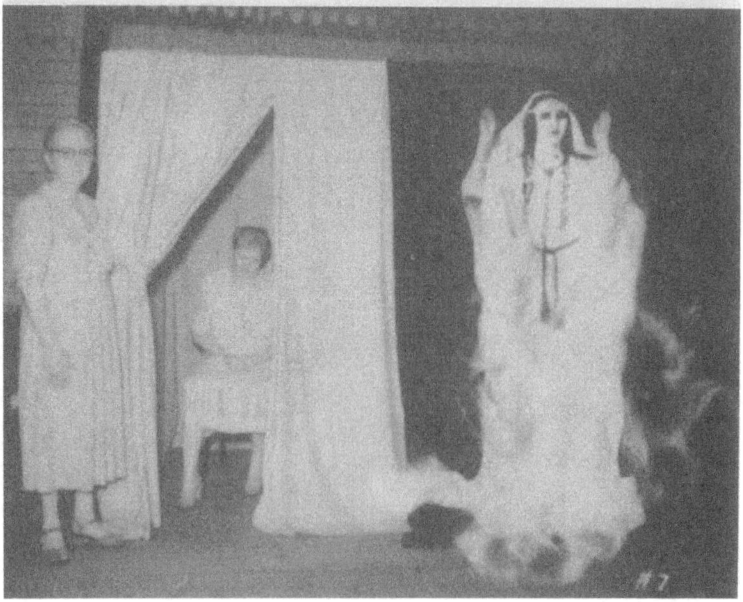
#7

Then came the catastrophe, "the direst and blackest that could overtake his mother and myself. The date of it," said the father, "is for ever burned into our souls. It made our lives without purpose, vain, and a mockery to us. We were desolated, heartbroken and inconsolable. Our yearning for him was an unbearable anguish.

"In a month, my hair had turned white and my physical condition was rapidly deteriorating. The thought that tormented me most was embodied in a gnawing doubt of his continued existence. What if he had been extinguished for ever? My fine lad no more! This thought kept me in a continual frenzy and panic."

He added that when the coffin containing his son's body was lowered into the ground he thought, "If this is the end, I don't want to go on." In the days that followed, he spent hours in the cemetery, in the wintry bitterness of December, unable to keep away from the grave. Here I would like to indicate what I later learned was the nature of the tragedy. This, his only, son, aged twenty-five, was accidently killed by electrocution at his fiancée's twenty-first birthday party. It was such a shock to her that she died three weeks later. Her memorial card read, "Laid to rest by the side of her fiancé". Their funeral services, within twenty-three days of one another, were held in the same church, with the same lesson and the same hymns.

If only, thought the grief-torn man, he could get some evidence of his son's continued existence, it might ease their anguish. He had been to four Spiritualist meetings during his life, but none of them had impressed him. The third was a demonstration of clairvoyance by Helen Hughes. He remembered saying afterwards that it was a very good performance of something, but of what he did not know.

Now he determined to visit a medium. He recalled that in his town a man, who was a stranger to him, had contributed several letters on Spiritualism to the press. In desperation he telephoned him without saying who he was.. He asked if he could suggest the name of any medium who could be seen forty to fifty miles away. The man at the other end of the line could not suggest anyone, but he said his wife might be able to help.

She was brought to the telephone, but could fare no better, except to refer the caller to another friend of hers, giving the telephone number. The distraught parent telephoned her. She again referred him to another friend in Leeds and gave her telephone number. This woman, in turn, supplied him with the telephone number of the secretary of the Leeds Society for Psychic Research. Another telephone call and he was speaking to the secretary, who arranged for a sitting with Helen Hughes. When the father was asked for his name, he replied that he preferred to remain anonymous. The secretary said he quite understood, and booked the séance as "anonymous".

The chief character in this story, as he afterwards told me, lived in Sheffield. With his wife he drove to Leeds, some forty miles away, and left their car in a station yard so that its registration number could give, no clue to his identity. Moreover, he went alone to the séance because he feared that inadvertently his wife might disclose some information. He travelled by tram to the 'Hyde Park district of Leeds, to the house where Helen Hughes was staying and where she was giving her séances.

The woman who opened the door was a complete stranger

to him, as he was to her. She showed him into a room, gave him a newspaper to read and a seat by the fire, saying that Mrs Hughes had somebody with her, but she would not be long. Presently she returned to say that Mrs Hughes was ready, and led him to another room where the medium walked across to meet him.

Now came the crucial moment. As she led, him to a settee, she said: "A very strong influence has come into the room with you . . . a bright, tall, fine boy and he's your son. What a wonderful boy! With him there comes an odour of a hospital, chloroform, or something."

Then, looking up and glancing sideways at a figure that only she could see, the medium added: "No, no, Doctor, I know the smell is not connected with your accident." Next, she turned to the father and added: "He says he had an accident which should never have happened and in a flash he was gone."

More information followed: "He says you have come quite a way to meet him. But you needn't have done so. He has never left you and has come in the car with you today." Again, there was an aside as she repeated: "Forty miles, you say, from R. . . ." The father's heart sank because he thought she was going to say the name of a town beginning with "R". But the medium went on: "No, no, Doctor, I hear you—Sheffield."

Here I quote the father's own words: "Could any reasonable man have resisted such a revelation? Could any proof be more compelling, or demonstration more convincing?" The remainder of the evidence, he said, was even more wonderful but of such a personal and intimate nature as to prevent him telling it publicly. He did, however, disclose one incident. The medium said: "He's getting excited about something belonging to him that is in your inside pocket."

The father emptied his inside jacket pocket. Beyond a driving licence, insurance certificate and another document, there was nothing, and he said so. "Yes, he insists," said the medium. The visitor suddenly thought of his overcoat on the settee beside him. He felt in the inside pocket. There was a silk handkerchief which had belonged to his son.

A few weeks later, he decided that there was no point in withholding his name any longer. It had now been revealed by so many mediums, as had been that of his son. Father and son had the same name—Dan Bradbury. I am glad to relate that he had the courage of his convictions. When he was asked to preside at a public Spiritualist meeting in Sheffield's largest hall, where he was well known and respected, he consented.

"The last place where some of my friends would expect to see me is on a Spiritualist platform," he declared. "Some of them are saying, 'Poor old Dan, he's gone crackers.' I do not mind. My one qualification for being here is that Mrs Helen Hughes provided me with proof of my son's survival." The medium was demonstrating clairvoyance that night.

What Dan Bradbury's friends did not know was that, without the evidence from Helen Hughes, it is likely that he would have "gone crackers", as he himself freely admitted.

Chapter 10
THE MOVING FINGER WRITES

IS the phenomenon of automatic writing evidence of activity from the spirit world, or can it be explained by the working of the subconscious mind? The real answer is to be found in the contents of the writing. If these disclose nothing supernormal and consist merely of "messages" whose purport is known to the medium, then it is reasonable to believe that the subconscious mind is responsible for their production. If, however, they reveal knowledge that the medium does not possess, then you must look for another explanation. It is always a safe rule in Spiritualism never to accept anything as having a spirit origin if a normal explanation will fit all the facts.

Geraldine Cummins, a non-professional medium, is the greatest living exponent of automatic writing. Through her hand there have come hundreds of thousands of words, much of it in superb prose, which amplify and continue the New Testament. Part of this writing, The Scripts of Cleophas, which supplements the Acts of the Apostles, was pronounced as "veridically evidential" by Doctor W. E. Osterley, who was Examining Chaplain to the Bishop of London, and an acknowledged expert on the Bible. Some scripts were produced in the presence of noted clergymen, including Dr Percy Dearmer, who was Canon of Westminster, Doctor Maud, then Bishop of Kensington, and the Canons of Bristol and Canterbury Cathedrals.

I have watched the seemingly incredible performance as

Miss Cummins acted as automatist for this form of mediumship. She sat at a table with numbered sheets of ruled paper in front of her. Her eyes were shaded with the left hand, while the elbow rested on the small table. In her right hand she held a fountain pen poised above the paper. In a few seconds the pen became galvanised and moved at the rate of 1,500 words an hour.

On her right sat Miss E. B. Gibbes, her great friend, whose presence seemed to act as a stimulant to Miss Cummins' mediumship. While the writing was being done, Miss Gibbes steadied the sheets of paper with both hands. The only time she guided the pen was when each page was completed. Then she placed a fresh sheet before Miss Cummins and the remorseless, speeding pen continued to write.

For over an hour the three of us, Miss Gibbes, the medium and I, sat in silence, broken occasionally by a whispered "Yes" or "No" from Miss Gibbes. I witnessed the production of writing from one of the medium's guides and from Frederick W. H. Myers, the distinguished classical scholar who was a convinced Spiritualist. Myers continued an essay started at a previous séance. It covered nine pages of foolscap paper and was written in beautiful prose as if it were all one word. With great rapidity the pen moved to the edge of the paper, never slipping, although the medium could not see.

The production of Miss Cummins' scripts takes two forms. In one of them she hears every word "spoken" by an inner "voice" and puts it down on paper. In the other phase, she passes into a light trance, and the writing is mechanically produced.

Miss Cummins is one of eleven children of a Professor of

Medicine at Cork University. Because of the fierce theological quarrels that she heard in Ireland, she turned her back on religion in her youth. She was an agnostic from the day that she was able to think for herself. Her support of a Suffragette at an open-air meeting led to her being stoned in the streets of Cork by an infuriated mob. She has played hockey for Ireland and is also a tennis enthusiast. Her chief interests have been drama and modern literature.

Because she wanted to become a writer, she left home for Dublin. She lived in the house of Hester Dowden, also a professor's daughter, only to discover that her hostess was a famous writing medium. Soon she realised that she possessed a similar gift, which Mrs Dowden helped her to develop.

Geraldine Cummins has never studied theology, philosophy, psychology, science, or Christianity's origins. Although she has read a great deal, her reading has been restricted largely to the works of modern writers. Neither she nor Miss Gibbes, who was present when all the automatic scripts dealing with Bible days were produced, has ever visited Egypt or Palestine.

For many years it has been a source of fascination to Miss Cummins to compare the scripts which come at her séances with her own work as an authoress. She has written a novel and is part-author of two Irish folk plays that were produced at the Abbey Theatre, Dublin. In her own literary work, Geraldine Cummins finds that her composition is always very slow. For this normal writing she produced six or seven hundred words in two days, and confesses that it is a laborious task. On reading the results she has to make many corrections.

When, however, she is the medium for automatic writing, the material flows from her pen without a pause or a correction. Although no i's are dotted or t's crossed, the script is always legible, intelligible and sequential. Frequently, at séances lasting an hour and a half, she has produced over 2,200 words. It is not surprising that she appears exhausted at the end of the session.

Her séance scripts dealing with the New Testament era have been subjected to the scrutiny of experts. Two of them were Professor W. P. Paterson, Professor of Theology, Edinburgh University, and Professor David Morison, Professor of Moral Philosophy, St Andrew's University. The verdict of the experts was that all the details of geography, history and terminology, where they can be checked, are unquestionably accurate. These two professors and Dr Osterley were responsible for a highly critical "Introduction" to The Scripts of Cleophas, from which I will quote. In it they say they have "satisfied themselves as to the genuineness and disinterestedness of the part played by Miss Cummins".

The scripts are said to be communicated by a highly complicated process. The actual transmission comes through the "Messenger", who avers that he is not the author. He asserts that the communications are made "at the bidding of Cleophas, who is too far removed from man to commune with him". The Messenger states that the chronicle, since published under the title of The Scripts of Cleophas, was known in the early Church. Only a few copies existed, however, and these have perished.

He declares that Cleophas, who is said to be a Christian convert of the first century, draws from more chronicles than one, and that his function is to fashion the whole of them into a single narrative. First, Cleophas has to draw on his memory, then impart the information to the one he calls the "Scribe", who transmits it to the Messenger, who "enters the mind" of the medium (he calls her "the handmaiden"), to find words to clothe what he has received. In view of this complicated process it is remarkable that the result is so lucid a document.

The Messenger has stated that the original writings from which the script is drawn were put together between sixty and seventy years after the birth of Jesus, though certain portions are of a slightly later date. Their authors, he asserts, were men who had themselves seen and heard the Apostles and who wrote mostly at Ephesus or Antioch, using either Greek or, less frequently, Aramaic or Hebrew.

The experts responsible for the published "Introduction" to The Scripts of Cleophas say that these supplement the Acts of the Apostles and St Paul's Epistles to the extent that they furnish an account of the Early Church and the Apostles from immediately after the death of Jesus to Paul's departure from Berea for Athens. They say: "This account shows signs of independence of the Scripture narrative, and does not appear to be based upon it or even to owe it much. The 'Messenger' is not apparently conscious of the existence of the Holy Writ, and declares, 'I have not the knowledge of those parts of the Holy Writings that have been preserved.'"

They add that the scripts contain material "which both supplements and explains what we know from the New Testament, and, moreover, supplies information which the Bible furnishes either incompletely or not at all". For example, the experiences of Paul after his conversion are described in details that do not appear in the New Testament.

These scholars point out that the incidents narrated in the first twelve chapters of the Acts of the Apostles occupy, all told, only some thirty separate days, while the chapters themselves cover a period of nine years at the very least. Thus, they say, it is easy to see that an immense portion of apostolic history has escaped record by the biblical historians.

They are satisfied that Miss Cummins cannot be the author, pointing out, for instance, that "only an unusually careful and profound student could have been responsible for giving to the head of the Jewish community in Antioch his accurate title of 'Archon'. Not long before the time when, presumably, the chronicle of Cleophas was written, the head of the Jewish community was called the Ethnarch, but when the organisation and government of the cities was altered by the Emperor Augustus in A.D. I 1, the title of the head of the Jewish communities was changed from Ethnarch to Archon.

"It would have been a pardonable error if the chronicle had used the title Ethnarch instead of Archon, especially as the writer lived in Palestine, where the Jews were ruled by the Sanhedrin; but the use of the comparatively new title Archon is an example of that exact knowledge on the part of the writer which is to be found in many other striking details only noticeable, perhaps, to those who are themselves authorities. Over and above this detailed knowledge, there are examples of insight which would appear to suggest a contemporary. The characters of the twelve apostles are described with an understanding and sympathy which is remarkable."

The fascinating account has been continued in other books, particularly in When Nero was Dictator, which describes how Paul spent the last years of his life, concerning which the Bible is silent. It takes up the threads at the point where the Acts of the Apostles leaves off and, in matchless language, carries on to the closing scenes of Paul's final days on earth. It describes his visit to Spain, his plans for the conversion of the Britons, and his last meeting with Peter in Rome. There is a brilliant picture of the court of Nero, with details of the intrigues of those days, culminating in an outstanding account of the burning of Rome.

Geraldine Cummins is a living refutation of the allegation that nothing of any value has been received through automatic writing. Her psychic gifts have thrown a new light on the Bible, made the obscure intelligible, and provided information which scholars had sought for years.

* * *

Hester Dowden, the writing medium who helped to develop Geraldine Cummins's psychic powers, used two methods to obtain her communications, a ouija board and a pencil. The ouija board owes its name to the combination of the two words, one French and the other German, which mean "Yes". A pointer, on a highly polished wooden surface, moves to letters of the alphabet.

When Mrs Dowden used the ouija board, messages were spelt out in lightning fashion, and normally the communicators gave their names and information of a highly individual character. Her guide seemed to take a delight in providing evidence of the kind that would confound sceptics. I once sent a lawyer to have some séances with Mrs Dowden. He came specially from Jamaica, 4,000 miles away, to try to obtain proofs of an afterlife. Although his father was the Archbishop of the West Indies, he had been an agnostic for years, a situation which did not conduce to harmony in the home.

At the lawyer's first séance, he received communications which, he said, were characteristic of the one person he hoped would return to him. In four weeks, at sittings with Hester Dowden, he obtained over one hundred items of evidence which clearly proved to him, as a lawyer, that life continued beyond the grave.

Mrs Dowden was also highly successful in "proxy séances". People living abroad would send her objects, which she held as a means of receiving communications for their owners. Invariably, after perusing the séance information, they confirmed the evidential nature of these messages. You can judge how convincing her séances must have been when I tell you that she gave over thirty thousand in thirty years of mediumship.

To watch one of her Ouija board séances was an unforgettable experience. Messages would arrive at a speed of three thousand words an hour—and bear in mind that each word had to be spelt out. When she used her pencil for automatic writing, the rate was reduced to a mere 2,500 words an hour. The majority of people will find that a thousand words an hour is as much as they can manage. It was not unusual for Hester Dowden to receive messages in foreign languages, in French and German, which she knew, and in Spanish, of which she was ignorant.

The most striking communications that came through her

hand were those claiming to originate from Oscar Wilde. Wilde's spirit signature was an exact replica of his earthly one. The handwriting disclosed his peculiarities. Events from his childhood days were mentioned and inquiry proved them to be accurate. The literary style, which is the acid test, was highly characteristic.

It all began at a séance one night with the words: "Lily, my little Lily. No, the lily was mine—crystal thread—a silver reed that made music in the morning."

"Who are you?" they asked. Immediately the writing began again: "Pity Oscar Wilde—one who, in the world, was a king of life. Bound to Ixion's wheel of thought, I must complete for ever the circle of my experience. Long ago I wrote that there was twilight in my cell and twilight in my heart, but this is the (last?) twilight of the soul.

"In eternal twilight I move, but I know that in the world there is day and night, seed time and harvest, and red sunset must follow apple-green dawn. Every year, spring throws her green veil over the world and anon the red autumn glory comes to mock the yellow moon. Already the may is creeping like a white mist over lane and hedgerow, and year after year the hawthorn bears blood-red fruit after the white death of its may."

Asked, "Why have you come here?" he replied: "To let the world know that Oscar Wilde is not dead. His thoughts live on in the hearts of all those who, in a gross age, can hear the flute voice of beauty calling on the hills or mark where her white feet brush the dew from the cowslips in the morning. Now the mere memory of the beauty of the world is an exquisite pain.

"I was always one of those for whom the visible world

existed. I worshipped at the shrine of things seen. There was not a blood-stripe on a tulip or a curve on a shell, or a tone on the sea, that but had for me its meaning and its mystery and its appeal to the imagination. Others might sip the pale lees of the cup of thought, but for me the red wine of life. Pity Oscar Wilde. To think of what is going on in the world is terrible for me. Soon the chestnuts will light their white candles and the foxgloves flaunt their dappled, drooping bells."

Then when the writing went on: "Soon the full moon will swim up over the edge of the world and hang like a great golden cheese," the words, "Stop, stop," were interjected. "This image is insufferable," the writing continued. "You write like a successful grocer who from selling pork has taken to writing poetry. I find the words in my medium's mind."

This gives an indication of how difficult it must be for a great literary craftsman to express himself through a medium. He went on: "Try again—'like a great golden pumpkin hanging in the night'." The second time, he found the words he wanted.

A week later, the automatic writing was resumed again. Dr E. J. Dingwall, then research officer of the Society for Psychical Research, was present. Wilde, the cynic and merciless satirist, expressed himself thus: "Being dead is the most boring experience in life. That is, if one excepts being married or dining with a schoolmaster. Do you doubt my identity? I am not surprised, since sometimes I doubt it myself. I might retaliate by doubting yours.

"I have always admired the Society for Psychical Research. They are the most magnificent doubters in the world. They are never happy until they have explained away their spectres. And one suspects a genuine ghost would make them exquisitely uncomfortable. I have sometimes thought of founding an academy of celestial doubters . . . which might be a sort of Society for Psychical Research among the living. No one under sixty would be admitted, and we should call ourselves the Society of Superannuated Shades. Our first object might well be to insist on investigating at once into the reality of the existence of, say, Mr Dingwall.

"Mr Dingwall, is he romance or reality? Is he fact or fiction? If it should be decided that he is fact, then, of course, we should strenuously doubt it. Fortunately there are no facts over here. On earth, we could scarcely escape them. Their dead carcases were strewn everywhere on the rose path of life. One could not pick up a newspaper without learning something useful. In it were some sordid statistics of crime or disgusting details relating to the consumption of pork that met the eyes; or we were told with a precision that was perfectly appalling and totally unnecessary what time the moon had decided to be jealous and eclipse the sun."

Is there any literary man who could sit down and produce spontaneously similar writing at the rate of sixty to seventy words a minute, which is the speed at which the Wilde communications came? In one instance, 1,700 words, a long and logical argument, were written in about an hour and a quarter.

Wilde criticised, as he did in his earth life, other writers: "I knew Yeats very well, a fantastical mind, but so full of inflated joy in himself that his little cruse of poetry was emptied early in his career. A little drop of beauty that was spread only with infinite pains over the span of many years."

"Time will ruthlessly prune Mr Wells's fig trees," was another phrase. "As for Mr Arnold Bennett, he is the assiduous apprentice to literature, who has conjured so long with the wand of his master Flaubert that he has really succeeded in persuading himself and others that he has learnt the trick. But Flaubert's secret is far from him. Of his characters, one may say that they never say a cultured thing and never do an extraordinary one. They are, of course, perfectly true to life—as true as a bad picture. Of late, we understand, he has taken to producing prostitutes.

"It is pleasanter to turn to Mr Eden Phillpotts, who, unlike Mr Bennett, on whose sterile pages no flowers bloom or birds sing, has a real and unaffected love of Nature, and, unfortunately, all Nature's lack of variety. He is a writer who has been very faithful, far too faithful, to his first love. One wishes that spring would sometimes forget to come to Dartmoor.

"I always had a kindly feeling towards poor Shaw. He had such a keen desire to be original that it moved my pity. He is so anxious to prove himself honest and outspoken that he utters a great deal more than he is able to think. He cannot analyse. He is merely trying to overturn the furniture and laughs with delight when he sees the canvas bottoms of the chairs he has flung over. He is ever ready to call upon his audience to admire his work; and his audience admires it from sheer sympathy with his delight. "The only mind I have entered into which appeals to my literary sense is John Galsworthy. He is my successor, in a sense. For although he dives more deeply into the interior of the human being, he is ever occupied with the exterior, which is so important in the play of society."

In this fashion, for pages and pages, Wilde wrote, at a speed which I am certain no "living" person could duplicate, perfect phrasing and biting criticism. Those who have read Salome may be interested in this passage:

"Like blind Homer, I am a wanderer. Over the whole world I have wandered, looking for eyes by which I might see. At times it is given me to pierce this strange veil of darkness, and, through eyes from which my secret must be for ever hidden, gaze once more on the gracious day. I have found sight in the most curious places. Through the eyes out of the dusky face of a Tamal girl I have looked on the tea fields of Ceylon, and through the eyes of a wandering Kurd I have seen Ararat and the Yezedes, who worship both God and Satan and who love only snakes and peacocks.

"Once on a pleasure steamer on its way to St Cloud I saw the green waters of the Seine and the lights of Paris, through the vision of a little girl who clung weeping to her mother and wondered why. Ah! those precious moments of sight. They are the stars of my night, the gleaming jewels in my casket of darkness, the priceless guerdon for whose sake I would willingly barter all that fame has brought me, the nectar for which my soul thirsts. Eyes! What can it profit a man if he loses them, or what can a man give in exchange for them? They are fairer than silver, better than seed pearls or many-hued opals. Fine gold may not buy them, neither can they be had for the wishes of kings. . . ."

Hester Dowden also received in automatic writing a play that was said to emanate from Oscar Wilde. Without disclosing the spirit authorship, she showed it to some theatrical managers. They all rejected it, she told me, one giving as his reason that it was too much like Oscar Wilde!

* * *

A highly intriguing aspect of automatic writing is cross-correspondence, in which messages, given in part to different mediums, separated by many miles, form a sequential communication when pieced together. Margery Crandon, one of the greatest mediums Spiritualism has ever produced, demonstrated for me a phase of cross-correspondence when my wife and I were her guests in America.

People who think that mediums are weird and uncanny must have been surprised to meet her. She was completely normal in outlook, a good sport, with a very happy disposition.

We witnessed the wide range and versatility of her mediumship for which, during the whole of her psychic career, she never charged a penny. In making this comment, I add that I see nothing reprehensible in a professional medium charging for her services. Mediums, like every other member of the community, must eat, pay rent, wear clothes and have money for all the essential requirements of life.

The argument, which I regard as fallacious, is sometimes offered that there should be no payment made where spiritual gifts are involved. The advocates of this viewpoint do not explain how the individuals concerned are to exist. They must either be paid, subsidised, or be made the recipients of charitable awards. A clergyman performing spiritual functions has to be paid, and rightly so. Calling it a stipend does not alter the principle.

In an ideal state, the possessors of spiritual gifts would not have to worry about their maintenance, but under present economic circumstances mediums have to live like everybody else. I mention that Margery Crandon never charged for her services because of the obvious criticism that where money is involved there could be the temptation to commercialise gifts, and even to cheat.

She and her husband, who had a distinguished medical career in Boston, must have been thousands of pounds out of pocket through her mediumship. They financed many of the scientific apparatuses which were designed to test her psychic powers. Their hospitality was proverbial, for they kept open house. Scientists, lawyers, authors, clergymen, doctors, conjurers and psychical researchers were among the guests who eagerly attended the Crandons' séances.

Margery Crandon was the centre of controversy which raged round her mediumship for years. The storms never seemed to touch her. She remained almost detached and would not even listen to a word of criticism against her detractors. Neither would she speak ill of them.

Her interest in Spiritualism was aroused after her husband had read some séance experiments conducted by Professor Crawford at Belfast. Dr Crandon was so intrigued that he wondered whether he could obtain similar results in his own home. At a series of regular séances, they discovered that his wife was the medium. The first to communicate was her Canadian brother, Walter Stinson, who was killed in a railway accident. After Walter had proved his survival in ways that left no doubt of his identity and Dr Crandon was not easy to convince—he became the presiding spirit genius at all his sister's séances.

First they had elementary psychic phenomena, consisting of movements of the table and messages spelt out by knockings and rappings. Later there came trance, the direct voice, the production of ectoplasm, materialisation, the passing of matter through matter, automatic writing, some of it in foreign languages, and cross-correspondence.

The evidence was cumulative. While at first there might have been an alternative explanation for one phase of the phenomena, taken as a whole it became clear to them that the intelligence of Walter was directing the results. One significant feature was the fact that he would announce beforehand the results that would later be obtained, thus demonstrating that there was intention at work.

One day Walter asked, "What more proof do you require?" He was told that fingerprints were regarded as irrefutable evidence of identity. Walter asked them to provide wax and hot water in the séance room, and thumb-prints, which he said belonged to him, began to arrive. They were able to confirm these with part of Walter's thumbprint found on a razor he had used shortly before his death.

Not satisfied, however, the indefatigable Walter introduced variations. At first the spirit thumbprints were positive, which is the normal result. These were followed by negative thumbprints, a physical "impossibility", for it meant that the ridges became indentations and the indentations became ridges. The next stage was to produce another "impossibility", negative thumbprints which were both convex and concave. Finally Walter complicated matters with mirror thumbprints, so that while they corresponded with the others, ridge for ridge, and indentation for indentation, they were reversed.

All these thumbprints, which he produced 131 times, showed, when enlarged, perfect details of normal skin anatomy, sweat glands and characteristic loops and whorls, as confirmed by police officials in Washington, Boston, Berlin, Munich, Vienna and Scotland Yard. At all the séances when the thumbprints were obtained, precautions were taken to immobilise the medium. Her ankles and wrists were lashed. She sat in an open cabinet, usually a recess or corner of the room, with her hands thrust through "portholes". Margery Crandon, who endured all these tests without complaint, agreed to being searched before and after her séances, and even consented to having a one-piece suit sewn on her, and then to being roped and tied to her chair with surgical tape.

It was once suggested to Walter that his thumbprint bore a resemblance to that of a living man. This was not really an argument against the supernormality of his results, but an allegation that fingerprints were not an infallible proof of identity. Walter's answer was to reproduce both his hands in wax.

It was because I knew all this background that I was delighted when Walter, at an impromptu séance, suggested that we have a test of cross-correspondence. One of the guests that night was Captain John W. Fife, head of Boston's naval dockyard. Walter asked Captain Fife to select six people, who were to choose a word or object the next night at 7 p.m. Then, said Walter, he would try to convey this word or object to Margery Crandon and to Sary Litzelman, another Boston medium who obtained her results by automatic writing.

Captain Fife was starting the next morning on an automobile trip with his children. He knew he would be motoring through New Hampshire, but he had no idea where he would be at 7 p.m. Nevertheless, he promised to find a group to select a word or object, and to get them to sign a statement telling what they had done. We arranged with Captain Fife that after this choice had been made, he would telephone French's Store at Royalston, about seventy miles from Boston, and give this word or object to them.

Margery Crandon had a country place, which was a collection of cabins in a forest, about a mile from Royalston. The next morning this medium, my wife, William H. Button, then president of the American. Society for Psychical Research, and I left for Royalston. Sary Litzelman and her husband were already staying in one of the forest cabins. None of these cabins had a telephone. French's Store was chosen because it was the nearest place with a telephone. When we arrived at Royalston I called and saw the manager, a Mr Wilcox, and asked him to note any message he received by telephone soon after 7 p.m. and I would later collect it.

At 7.10 p.m. Margery Crandon sat in one cabin, and Sary Litzelman in another, with no possible means of normal communication between them. In the presence of Mr Button, her Japanese servant and myself, Margery Crandon wrote the words "Water Melon". Sary Litzelman, in the presence of my wife, wrote the same words. Incidentally, Mrs Litzelman's communications were always received in mirror writing, which meant that you had to hold them to a looking-glass before you could read them. While Margery Crandon was writing, the Japanese servant was playing with her dog, making it growl. The medium told it to stop, but the distraction made no apparent difference to her writing.

I went by car to French's Store and collected from Mr Wilcox the message he had received by telephone a few minutes earlier. He handed me a sealed envelope. Inside it, on a slip of paper, I found written "Water Melon". Later I obtained a signed statement from all who had participated in this psychic experiment. Mr Button, who had been concerned in several similar experiments, told me that they succeeded only when mooted by Walter, or conducted with his approval.

During my visit, Margery Crandon gave a demonstration of her ability to name correctly the denominations of playing-cards that she could not see. It was Mr Button who suggested the idea. He had been reading about similar experiments conducted by Professor J. B. Rhine which had attracted world-wide comment. Mrs Crandon agreed to a trial, but refused to regard it as a serious matter. She took part in it in snatches as she came from the kitchen into the dining-room, where we sat, during her preparations for lunch.

In the Pullman coach from New York, Mr Button, a distinguished corporation lawyer, had bought two new packs of playing-cards. These were handed to me and I broke the seals. The two packs, I noted, had a similar design on the backs of the cards. From them I chose twenty-five cards, aces, kings, queens, knaves and tens. One by one I held up each card, its back to the medium, seven feet away, while my wife, Mr Button, Captain Fife and I looked at the faces of the cards.

Margery Crandon named twenty-one cards correctly without any hesitation. The four she missed were all tens. Of these, two were wrongly named, but on her own recall she designated them correctly, in one case on the second attempt, and the other on the third. These corrections were voluntary on her part, with no prompting from any of us.

The tens seemed to be the ones that caused difficulty. I took the five tens, placed them together in the middle of the other twenty cards. This time the medium was fifteen feet away. Margery Crandon immediately named twenty-four cards correctly, including four of the tens. The fifth ten she called wrongly at first, but immediately corrected herself. For this experiment, my wife held up the cards with their backs to the medium, while Mr Button, Captain Fife and I looked on.

When we congratulated the medium on this striking success, she answered, with a laugh, that there was nothing to it. It was so easy, she added, that she proposed to "switch the influence" to my wife. While under this alleged influence, my wife succeeded in attaining a high degree of accuracy in naming unseen cards, producing results that were far and away beyond those that would come from chance. I cannot pretend to explain what this "influence" was. All I know is that on many occasions since that day I have repeated the experiment with my wife, but the results never exceeded those that are obtained by chance.

Chapter 11
MEDIUMS ARE BORN

IT is all very well, you may say, to narrate these examples of psychic phenomena, but how does a medium discover that she is a medium? Is there some pattern common to them? There is, as you will see, and the evidence is that they are born with a latent gift.

Estelle Roberts, perhaps the most versatile of all mediums, had her first psychic experience when she was eight years old. She does not retain a pleasant memory of the incident, for it resulted in her being severely reprimanded by an angry father for telling untruths. In a room on the third floor of their house, she and her elder sister were getting ready for school. The two children were surprised to hear three taps on the window. Simultaneously the room darkened. It seemed as if a heavy cloud had cast a shadow on the window.

Young Estelle, startled, looked up. Afraid that the sight which met her eyes might terrify her sister, she cried: "Don't look!" Of course, her sister looked—and promptly fainted. Estelle was glued to the spot by a vision of a knight in shining armour. He appeared to be suspended in space, outside the window. A glistening sword was in his outstretched hand. His visor was thrown back. Though more than half a century has passed, Estelle Roberts can still recall his striking features. His deeply penetrating eyes searched those of the young medium, to whom he beckoned. The next moment he had vanished.

Having heard her sister's scream, the father rushed upstairs. When Estelle excitedly related what she had seen, he scolded her for inventing so fantastic a story. "What you saw must have been a bat," was his crushing answer. But Estelle Roberts has always regarded this curious psychic happening as an introduction of what was to become her life's mission. It was not until she reached middle age that the figure of the knight reappeared to her.

At school, Estelle was an average child, but she differed from her companions in one marked respect. She constantly heard "voices" and saw apparitions. Other children called her a dreamer, not realising that she was fascinated at listening to voices which nobody else could hear. When she mentioned this strange happening to her parents, who were good, sound church people, they accused her of suffering from too vivid an imagination.

Her first situation, at the age of fifteen, was that of a nursemaid. She hoped that the work could so occupy her mind that the strange manifestations would be excluded, but the voices still persisted, as did the visions. As she wheeled a child in the perambulator, the spirit forms seemed to follow her. She could hear them speaking. They told her of things she did not know, and that she could not even have guessed.

Not understanding that she possessed psychic powers, Estelle tried to suppress them. Gradually the realisation was forced on her that she was really different from other girls. In her ignorance, she was afraid that she might become insane. At seventeen she married and found a devoted husband, to whom she confided her fears. He was sympathetic, but knowing nothing about Spiritualism concluded that his young wife was "fey".

One night, as she lay in bed, she saw, clairvoyantly, a figure pass slowly across the room. Because she recognised the form, she said to her husband: "Your aunt is dead." With natural suspicion, he asked: "How can you possibly know?" She could not explain, except that she did. Early next morning a telegram arrived confirming the aunt's death the night before.

Then tragedy moved into her life. Her husband, never a strong man, became seriously ill. She had to work hard to support him and their three children. Her voices tried to cheer and comfort her, but it seemed as if they were the bearers of bad tidings. When she saw the spirit forms gathering round her husband's bed, she knew that the time had come for him to say farewell. She sent the children out of the house and sat alone with her husband, tending him in his last earthly hours. Psychically she had been told that he would not recover. She sat by the bedside awaiting the inevitable parting.

As it drew near, she saw two spirit forms sharing her vigil. They were her husband's parents. Quietly, as her husband drew his last breath, she noticed a thin, almost transparent cord which appeared to disengage itself slowly from his head. Gradually, a similar silk-like substance emerged from other parts of the body until, finally, the complete spirit form of her husband was visible to her. It appeared to be a separate and living replica of the body which lay on the bed. Slowly, this spirit body was removed from her vision. With it went the spirit doctors who had come to help her husband's passing to his new life. The parents, who had come to greet him, also disappeared.

There were few mourners at the funeral. Nobody offered

a word of comfort to the sorrowing young widow. She stood by the open grave a lonely, forlorn figure. Tears ran down her cheeks as she thought of their children and the bleak future that awaited them and herself. Encouragement came from an unexpected source. As the clergyman read the burial service, her eyes gazed at the grave. She was startled to see the spirit body of her husband hovering over the coffin. The vision was so clear that she could recognise his features. He smiled gently and encouragement seemed to flow from him, somehow conveying that she must not despair.

"Dust to dust, ashes to ashes," intoned the clergyman. The words did not worry her, for, she says: "I realised at that moment that my husband had not really left me." Though the experience brought consolation, there were still material problems to be faced—one was how to earn enough money to keep her children.

There followed a weary search for work. Eventually she found a job as a waitress in a cafe miles away. It was an arduous existence. She had to leave home at 7 a.m., and did not return until r 1 p.m. Every night, after the long day's toil, the tired widow had to prepare her family's meals for the next day. Though worn out with her exertions, her psychic power was still active.

"Every day," she says, "as with aching feet I tramped the cafe floor, I could hear my voices and see my visions. Behind the heads of the customers I served, I could see the forms of `guardian angels'. I could have given those customers something much more valuable than the sausages and chips most of them ate. Had I understood, I could have given them spiritual food."

Wisely she held her own counsel, realising that if she

had related her visions she would be regarded as crazy, and possibly lose her job. Even so, she still did not realise the true explanation, that she possessed mediumship. Then came what proved to be the turning-point. A neighbour invited her to attend a Spiritualist service. She was singled out by the clairvoyant, who said: "You are a born medium. You have great work to do in the world."

This was the first explanation she had received of her voices and visions. Nevertheless, before deciding to throw in her lot with the Spiritualists, she felt it essential that some psychic sign be vouchsafed to her. When she said so to the clairvoyant, who was an experienced medium, she was asked to follow a certain procedure. For an hour, on consecutive nights, Estelle Roberts was told to sit at a table. The sign she sought would then come. Mrs Roberts agreed to try the experiment. For six nights she sat faithfully, but nothing happened. Sceptical and somewhat irritated, she resumed her vigil on the seventh night. As the allotted hour ended, she stood up in disgust. "That's that," she said to herself. "It is the finish of Spiritualism as far as I am concerned."

Intending to go to her children's room, she walked towards the door. As she moved, she felt something pressing against the back of her neck. The pressure continued as she neared the door. Puzzled, she looked behind, to find the table at which she had been sitting was suspended in the air. One edge was actually touching her neck. She gazed at the spectacle of a table half-way between floor and ceiling, held steadily without any apparent support. As she watched, it moved back across the room, and descended gently to the floor in its original position.

Having heard that if hands were placed on the table,

messages were said to be rapped on it, she thought she would try the experiment. A message came by means of raps, using a code that had already been told her—one rap for "a", two for "b", three for "c", etc. The message was: "I, Red Cloud, come to work for humanity." This message was her first conscious link with her guide. It marked the beginning of a great co-operation which, in forty years, has brought comfort to thousands who were bereaved.

More dramas have been re-enacted in a cottage at Tankerton, on the Kentish coast, than on any stage in any theatre in the world. It is the home of Gladys Osborne Leonard, sometimes known as "The Queen of English mediums". In this small house, on many hundreds of occasions, there have been stirring reunions between the living and the dead. The artificial happenings of the stage fade into insignificance compared with the superb dramas when Life and Death play the leading characters. Curiously enough, Mrs Leonard experienced her first trance mediumship beneath the stage of the London Palladium when she was a touring actress.

She achieved fame through the public tributes paid to her mediumship by Sir Oliver Lodge. The renowned scientist, after attending, at first anonymously, many of her séances, was convinced that he had received indisputable communications from his son, Raymond, a victim of the First World War. He has recorded some of his evidence in Raymond and other books. It was through Mrs Leonard's psychic powers that Robert Blatchford, for years a Rationalist with an agnostic outlook that was almost militant, proved his wife's survival, a fact which compelled him to change the whole of his life's philosophy. Even so, he told me, for years afterwards he wondered whether "it is too good to be true". Chancellor R. J. Campbell, the distinguished divine, was also one of Mrs Leonard's regular sitters. After a long psychic quest, he declared that he had received through her séances his final proof of the afterlife.

When you meet Mrs Leonard she is so unassuming and reserved that you would find it hard to believe she is one of the world's greatest trance mediums. It all began when as a young child she had visions which nobody else could see. Every morning, soon after she awoke, while dressing, or having her nursery breakfast, beautiful scenes met her gaze. In whatever direction she looked, the walls, door or ceiling would disappear. In their place would gradually come valleys with gentle slopes, lovely banks and trees, and all around flowers of every colour and shape. The scene always seemed to extend for many miles.

She was conscious, though she could not explain why, that she could see much farther than was possible with the normal, physical scenery around her. Although she was too young to understand, she knew that she was looking at vistas that do not belong to this world. She can remember thinking to herself what a contrast there was between the scenery and people of her visions and those that came within the range of her normal sight.

The individuals of her visions were vastly different from what she called the "down here" people. They conveyed feelings of peace, light and love. There was never a sign of doubt, fear or mystery. "It all looked too expressive of love and joy," she says, "to be in any way connected with the unsatisfactory state in which I mentally lived." At the time she did not regard the visions as abnormal, or even unusual. Nevertheless, some instinct made her keep silent about them. She thought that everybody else around her saw these scenes, or similar ones, but did not appreciate them sufficiently or dwell upon their beauty as she did. While experiencing these visions she used to look at the faces of grown-ups who happened to be in the room, and was surprised to notice how uninteresting and wooden their expressions were despite the glories unfolded to their view.

One morning, as a special treat because her father was going to Scotland, she was allowed to go down
to breakfast instead of having it in the nursery. Bundled quickly out of bed and thrust into a dressing-gown, scarcely awake, she sat at the breakfast table gazing sleepily at the wall opposite her. Her favourite view of the "Happy Valley", the name she called it, began to appear. Instead of refraining from mentioning it, she said casually to her father: "Isn't that a specially beautiful place we are seeing this morning?"

"What place?" he asked. The youthful Gladys pointed to the dining-room wall, which was bare except for two guns hanging on it. "What are you talking about?" her father asked. Her attempt at explanation brought the whole family around her, all agitated, anxious and annoyed.

At first they maintained that she was fabricating, but they could not shake her persistence. She described many of her visions in such details that they were forced to conclude there was something in them, but whatever it was did not accord with their conventional way of looking at things. Her father sternly forbade her to have any more visions.

Psychic faculty comes naturally to many children, but, alas, too often has to be suppressed by parents who believe they are caused by hallucinations which require medical attention. Despite her father's prohibition, Gladys continued to have her visions, and to become on familiar terms with the people who appeared in them.

To the horror of her parents, she chose the stage for a career, and travelled with a repertory company. In one town she was attracted by a notice board which indicated a Spiritualist meeting, but she was not impressed when she visited it. Something urged her to make a second attempt.

This time she was singled out by the clairvoyant and given a spirit message from a cousin whose description she was speedily able to recognise. When she told her mother, expecting this news to be welcome, she was admonished with the request not to mention the subject again. Gladys related that part of the message was a prophecy that she was being prepared for a special work, but her mother was adamant in her refusal to be associated with Spiritualism.

Another spirit message foretold how Gladys would meet her husband. She found it difficult to accept the forecast because of the grotesque clothing and appearance of the man described to her. Appearing in a Whitstable theatre, she was dashing upstairs to make her entrance on the stage when she stumbled over a basket of props and fell headlong into the arms of the producer, who was coming downstairs. He, too, was playing a part in the production. The costume and make-up he wore exactly fitted the medium's description. As she lay in his arms he kissed her and she responded. "I knew I had come home," she says. Theirs was an ideally happy marriage until it was ended, in the earthly sense, by her husband's death following an injury to his back.

Meanwhile, backstage and in dressing-rooms up and down the country, Gladys Leonard and her friends used every available spare moment to sit for table-tipping séances. For the first twenty-six sessions there were no results. On the twenty-seventh there came a communication from one calling herself "Feda", who asserted that Gladys would become a trance medium. This made no appeal to the actress, but Feda said she could best work through her in trance. One curious sidelight about Feda is that she claims to be an ancestress of her medium.

Gladys Leonard was playing at the London Palladium. The dressing-rooms were crowded. She and her friends could not find a quiet place to hold a séance. One night, wandering about the theatre, when all seemed hopeless, they discovered a very steep, narrow staircase leading down from the stage. Though they had no right to do so, they climbed down the ladder.

They found themselves in a large, deserted room with engines and machinery that were used for heating, lighting and other purposes of the theatre. This seemed the ideal spot. There was nobody in sight. The walls and ceiling were so thick that they could hear very little except the muffled thud of the machinery. They discovered a clean corner, which seemed a peaceful haven after all the noise and clatter up above. Her husband, who had returned from the provinces and fortunately had been engaged for this production just before it opened, obtained a table and three chairs. They secreted them downstairs, desperately hoping they would not be discovered.

Between nine and ten o'clock every night, when they were not wanted on stage, they determined to hold their séances. They were delighted with the results. Feda spelt out messages, repeating every time that she was going to control

Mrs Leonard, but nothing happened. Her two friends, Agnes and Nellie, and her husband, maintained their enthusiasm, but Gladys Leonard became tired and impatient. The theatre, then a new one, had been built by Sir Walter Gibbons, who was managing director of the company which owned it. They knew nothing about him, and had never seen him until they came to the Palladium for this special production.

One evening, as usual, Mrs Leonard prepared herself for a dull session. Feda had given up spelling messages through the table, saying she wanted to concentrate entirely on controlling her medium. They noticed that Sir Walter, whom they had just begun to know by sight, had come down into the engine room and pacing backwards and forwards, with his hands clasped behind him. They had arrived a little earlier than usual, so they sat in silence hoping he would not notice them in the gloom. He glanced at them casually and, to their surprise, did not order them to clear out as they expected. Instead, occupied with his problem, he kept pacing up and down about fifty or sixty feet from where they sat. "Will he never go?" they thought.

While waiting, Mrs Leonard relapsed into what seemed an unusual sleepy state. She felt more pessimistic than ever about her alleged psychic powers. The drowsy, tired feeling increased. Lazily, she thought: "It's darker than usual tonight. I'm sleepy; they won't notice it if I sleep for a little while." She fell asleep. When she awoke, she could not have told whether she had been absent for hours or for minutes.

The scene that met her is indelibly engraved on her memory. Agnes and Nellie were leaning across the table, holding her hands. She noticed that they were agitated. When Nellie switched the light on, Gladys Leonard saw that tears were glistening on the cheeks of her two companions. "What on earth's the matter?" she asked. "Matter!" replied Agnes. "Feda has been controlling you and giving us spirit messages from our relatives. Nellie's mother has communicated. We have had a wonderful time."

In the spring of 1914, Feda said that a terrible disaster was going to happen to the world and that she hoped to help many people through Mrs Leonard. Though she was not attracted to the idea of becoming a professional medium, circumstances compelled her to adopt this course. Then came the war, with its tragedy of bereavement for thousands.

Gladys Leonard proved to be so successful as a medium that she speedily rose to fame. In fifty years of devoted service, to which she has subordinated all other activities, she has earned world-wide respect. Even hostile anti-Spiritualists and sceptical psychical researchers have praised her probity and her single-minded devotion to her mediumship.

One of the many people who sought her psychic aid in trouble, and who became a regular attendant at her séances, was Sir Walter Gibbons. He laughed when, after they became great friends, she reminded him of the first time they had ever met, beneath the stage of the Palladium.

Feda's forecast came true in a long and successful mission which has achieved the purpose of this seemingly ordained partnership. An outstanding feature of her séances for many years is the fact that sitters frequently hear Feda's voice speaking phrases or sentences before she repeats them through her entranced medium.

Mrs Leonard, whose early life was filled with visions of the other world, once had a curious out-of-the-body experience. In this astral journey she visited the room of a man who lay in great pain on his bed. For some unknown reason, she administered healing to him. As she was about to leave the room for the return journey home, she was seized with a fit of violent coughing. The next moment, she awoke with a start to find her husband in some anxiety over her very real paroxysm.

While she lay thinking about her astral experience, she realised that the man she had seen on the bed was Sir Arthur Conan Doyle. With some hesitation, she wrote to him, describing her nocturnal adventure. In reply, she received a telegram reading, "Please come immediately". When she arrived at his home, Sir Arthur told her that he had been desperately ill that night. The door had opened, and the figure of a woman came into the room. He added that this woman approached him and gave him healing treatment. "Then as she was leaving," he said, "I heard her have a violent fit of coughing!"

Mrs Leonard, whose mediumship has comforted thousands of mourners, had herself to face the acid test of bereavement. The angel of death visited her home and removed her beloved husband, who had been ill for years after enduring pain like a martyr. The widow showed no sign of distress because she regarded her husband's passing as a happy relief from suffering.

Then a unique event happened. Gladys Leonard gave herself a sitting. Wanting to hear from her husband, she arranged with her niece to record what would be said when she went into trance. Through the lips of the unconscious medium there came a series of intimate messages from her own husband, describing his new life and the relatives he had met, and ending with a message of love.

"I learnt a lot from my husband's passing," Mrs Leonard told me, "for he described in details his new adventure to me." It fortified her determination to continue the mediumship to which she had dedicated her life. It is fitting to quote her summary of the communications that have come through her psychic powers: "Never, in all the thousands of messages that I have known of during many years of work, have I heard one word that could have any but a helpful and ennobling influence on the character and mind of the recipient."

* * *

Like most mediums, Helen Shepherd had psychic experiences as a child. Because she was always "seeing things" her Methodist parents had secret fears about her sanity. When she, the first of seven children of a bottle-finisher in a glass works, described her invisible playmates, she was scolded for indulging in "absurd fancies", especially as she related how they came into the house though both front and back doors were locked.

No matter how many times she was reproved for "telling lies", Helen knew that she could see and hear real children, because she played with them. Even at school she was punished for her visions. Yet a number of other children shared one of her psychic experiences.

At the age of eleven she was going to morning school at Seaham Harbour. Passing through a doorway, she was attracted by a child, unlike any of those attending the school, standing by the window inside her classroom. Helen called about twelve other children and pointed to the figure by the window which, strangely, they all could see. They decided that the child must have been accidentally locked inside the school.

The teacher approached the chattering crowd to ask the reason for their excitement. They pointed to the window, but the child had disappeared. Their explanations did not convince the teacher, who selected Helen as the "ringleader" of a practical joke. As a punishment for "seeing a ghost", she made Helen stand by the same window where the vision had appeared.

There is a strange sequel to this childhood happening. Years later, after Helen Hughes, as she became through marriage, had given one of her typical brilliant demonstrations of clairvoyance in Glasgow, a woman came forward to congratulate her. She was the teacher who had punished her. Now, with some contrition, she declared: "Well, Helen Shepherd, to think that all this began with the ghost!"

About three years after the school incident, Helen had another strange psychic experience. Playing with her friends in the street, she looked up in the sky and clearly saw the words, "Fever spreading". This time none of the other children could see anything unusual. When Helen's mother heard this latest story, she rebuked the child. Yet three weeks later, Helen caught the fever.

Though soon afterwards Helen left school to start as an apprentice to a dressmaker, the visions and voices continued. At the early age of eighteen, she married Thomas Hughes, a miner. The responsibilities of a working woman's life, and the birth of three children in just under four years, seemed to force her psychic faculties into the background. After the birth of her last baby she developed a severe spinal complaint, and became an invalid with no immediate hope of recovery.

There followed the darkest days of her life. Added to her constant pain was the growing fear caused by the return of the strange psychic happenings which began to make her doubt her own sanity. There was no one to explain the simple fact that she was an undeveloped medium, not even a dramatic vision to make her realise that she had a mission to fulfil.

Helen Hughes had become so ill that she was expected to die. Relatives and friends gathered for what seemed the inevitable end. Instead, she found herself walking in a garden of dazzling beauty, profuse with flowers of all colours. To her surprise she met an elderly woman friend whom she knew to be long since dead. Excited by this reunion, they had a long discussion, in which Helen became conscious of a new lease of vigorous life in marked contrast to the miserable existence which had been her lot.

"After a few moments of conversation," Helen recalls, "I saw a flower that even in this garden of ineffable beauty seemed to outshine all in its brilliance of colour, and reached forward to caress it. But I was restrained with the words, Not yet, you have work to do."

She awoke to find her relatives and friends bending anxiously over her. Excitedly, she told them that she knew she was not going to die. Outwardly, they agreed; inwardly, they doubted. Her suffering was not over. For two years she was unable to walk and had to use a bath chair.

As she lay helpless and worn with pain, she began to hear the voices of people who she knew were long since dead, and she began to see them. This recurring experience alarmed her, and revived the fear that her sanity was breaking down under the long strain of illness. She was taken to many doctors, but none could help her.

Then her voices urged her imperatively: "Get up and walk." She could not walk at the time, but she tried. When she put her feet on the floor, she found that they had life in them, though they seemed to have been dead for a long time. The voices urged her to persevere. Concurrently, her health began to take a slow turn for the better.

When the doctor called she repeated what the voices had told her. He, believing that her mind might become un-hinged, advised her to go away for a rest. But Helen Hughes had become inspired with a growing confidence in her voices. She felt she had turned the corner. At first, she walked slowly, with the aid of sticks, but eventually she was able to discard them. As she became better, the voices grew stronger, louder, and were more frequent.

They were accompanied by other psychic phenomena, which were disconcerting. There were knockings on the wall, and her bed would shake. Now came another complication. She was regularly visited for months by the form of an unknown woman, whom she clearly saw, but who did not speak to her. The visitor came in and left by the door, but occasionally she seemed to vanish. Somehow, Helen Hughes knew that her visitor was no longer in this world.

She decided that the only way to end these sleepless nights was to leave their haunted house. With her husband she visited the colliery office to ask for another cottage. She described her experiences to an official who, unexpectedly, was helpful and understanding when she had anticipated ridicule. "Please don't think I am insane," she implored.

He was the first person to display real appreciation of her problem.

"You are not insane," he said, with a friendly smile. Turning to her husband, he added: "There is more in her little finger than in some people's whole bodies." Later, Helen Hughes discovered that he understood something of the subject because his wife was a Spiritualist, but, unfortunately, he did not refer to his knowledge.

He complied with their request and found them another cottage in Dawdon. If Helen Hughes believed that a change of home would also end the strange happenings she was soon undeceived. The phenomena were more insistent than ever. The change of house, however, brought one important, if unexpected, development. Thomas Hughes, who still jokingly insisted that "she was seeing things", began to see things himself. His doubts ended when he perceived the unknown woman who had presented herself to his wife for many months.

Then destiny played its trump card. It brought to the house an obscure but spiritually enlightened wayfarer who was to transform her life. One morning, after a disturbed night, there came three loud raps on the door. It was an old roadman who had been working outside. He asked if she would warm his can of tea at the fire. Helen invited him in.

She had an inexplicable urge to recount her strange experiences and confide in the old man. Her long recital included the fear of losing her reason, because she heard and saw the dead, and a mention of the persistent woman visitor.

He listened sympathetically, and exclaimed in his broad Durham dialect: "Why, hinney, you're the richest woman in Dawdon. Your visitor has come to help you and you are going to be a great medium." He urged on Helen Hughes that she should talk to the woman the next time she came, something she had never done. The roadman was a Spiritualist. In a few minutes he explained her mediumship and its purpose. "You are merely using an extra sense, one that is beyond the ordinary five," he said. "Second sight is what some people call it."

When he finished, Helen Hughes recalled an experience years earlier when there had been a hint of her psychic career without her realising it. A Norwegian sailor, who had come into a cafe which she helped to manage at Seaham Harbour, suddenly said to her: "Lady, you speak with angels. Your angel mother, Margaret, tells me she is helping you and your family." Apart from the fact that her mother's name was Margaret, and she thought it odd for the sailor to mention it, the realisation of what he said had not dawned on her. Now that the roadman had patiently and logically explained her strange phenomena, she felt she had reached the turning-point in her life.

For six months, the roadman came to see her daily, encouraging her in every way he could. Finally, he advised her to visit a Spiritualist church. She received a message from the visiting clairvoyant, a complete stranger, who knew all about her psychic experiences and predicted that she would become a great medium herself.

Helen Hughes now awaited with confidence a visit from the mystery woman. This time she greeted her and was met with the reply: "I am Willie Ducker's mother." Willie was well known to Helen because he lived in the same village. He was on active service and had been declared missing for several months. She had never known Mrs Ducker. The next morning, full of excitement, she got up to tell Willie's sister. When she arrived she was greeted with the news: "Our Willie's been killed." The tragedy had been conveyed to the sister in news brought only a few minutes before by the postman.

Chapter 12
SERMONS IN STONES

PSYCHOMETRY provides evidence that there are "sermons in stones". By this means inanimate objects are capable of divulging their history and revealing complete details of their surroundings and the people with whom these articles have been associated.

There are two schools of thought as to how psychometry, a Greek word meaning "soul measurement", is performed. The first maintains that it does not involve mediumship. It requires only a psychic ability to register emanations and conditions associated with the object. The second asserts that mediumship is entailed, because the psychometrist is relying on clairvoyance received from a guide or someone else in the Beyond associated with the object or its present owner. My view is that both explanations are possible and that they sometimes overlap.

The radiations from inanimate objects can be compared with the aura which surrounds a human being. To a trained clairvoyant, the colours in the aura give an accurate index of personality, character, health, inclinations, ambitions and the state of mental and spiritual progress. Similarly, an object yields its secrets to the expert psychometrist.

Science has familiarised us with the fact that what seems solid matter is in reality a series of frequencies, radiations or vibrations. Every object which has been in our possession is impregnated with our aura and retains these aural emanations. When a competent psychometrist handles any article, she is able to give a delineation of its history and all its associations. She receives the strongest impressions concerning the most recent owners. There are exceptions due to the fact that where great emotions, such as tragedy or drama, have been called into play these leave a greater impression upon the object.

Public demonstrations of psychometry are frequently given at Spiritualist meetings. The procedure is for an official to go among the audience with cards numbered in duplicate. Those who wish to have an article psychometrised take a numbered card, attach one portion to the object and retain the other for reference purposes. Great care is taken to avoid these articles touching one another and so leading to confusing delineations. The owner places his object on a specially constructed tray divided into compartments, each large enough to hold only one article. The medium picks up an object and gives the delineation, calling the number attached so that the person to whom it belongs can follow what is said.

Psychometry, when done by a highly expert exponent like Estelle Roberts, attains an accuracy that is remarkable for its detail. Here are some instances that came under my observation.

The medium chose a ring which she said had great antiquity. Its owner denied her statement, saying that she had casually bought it at an unimportant little trinket shop in Islington, North London. Undaunted, Estelle Roberts stated that the ring was valuable and its worth should have been recognised by experts long before it reached a little shop. She insisted that the stone in the ring was ancient, although the setting was modern. She was so confident that she advised the owner to check her statements. The woman decided to make it a test case and went to the British Museum, where expert opinion confirmed the accuracy of the medium's psychic impressions.

"You gave me a wonderful reading of a scarab ring," the owner, Edith Peck, wrote later to Mrs Roberts. "I promised to let you know the result of my visit to the British Museum to find out when the ring was first in existence. You remember I told you I was under the impression the ring was modern. They confirmed your statement that the gold was modern, but not the stone. The stone belongs to the 'Middle Kingdom', 1700 to 1800 B.C. There were many made at the time, and they were buried with the mummies. The hieroglyphics at the base are lotus flowers. They had some sacred meaning at, that time. The ring was a genuine scarab. It is wonderful you should get such a picture of the mummy, as I noticed several photographs in the Egyptian gallery like your description, and they were of the above date, the hair in rolls at the side of the face was as you described. I think, had the stone belonged to a king, his name would have been inscribed at the base of the ring, but probably you are correct about the priest. What I should like to know is how it came to be in a little jeweller's shop in Islington."

On another occasion, when Estelle Roberts was attracted to a flat piece of stone, she said: "I hope the person to whom this stone belongs knows its history. It has come a long distance. It was once part of a monastery or temple. The stone is very old. I see with it death—the trampling of feet, and blood conditions. More than one person has suffered. Am I correct?"

The member of the audience who had provided the stone

replied that these conditions were accurate, although the stone was part of an old castle. "It was taken out of the stonework," said the psychometrist. "Yes," replied the owner, "I removed it myself from the centre of the wall."

The medium continued: "Originally, there was an archway at the top of the wall. The building from which this was taken would be hundreds of years old. Many a battle was fought there. I see steel armour and helmets. I see a gap in the wall. Now the wall is being chipped by cannon. There are dead bodies lying on the ground. Nearby there should be a large stream of water." She paused. "Have you also another stone?" she asked. "That is perfectly true," came the reply.

Mrs Roberts added that the two pieces of stone had been kept together. From the vibrations of the object she held in her hand, she could piece together the story of the second stone. She had received the impression at first of a monastery or chapel. Obviously, it must have referred to the other portion of stone, for the medium said: "The second piece formed part of an ancient chapel in a different vicinity. I see that, at some period, royal persons stayed at the castle. One member even disappeared. Close to the stone's position was a battlement slit, used as a peephole, and also through it arrows were shot."

The owner excitedly replied: "I took that stone from a royal castle in North Wales which is reputed to be the birthplace of Prince Llewellyn."

Estelle Roberts gave the history of another object chosen from the tray, this time a brooch. "This brooch has been worn by two people," she said. "It has been pinned on a dark plush cushion. One wearer used to fasten it in a pretty piece of lace, which was bunched round the neck. Also I see someone studying very deeply. I sense a mind which considers everything thoroughly, a person who is just becoming associated with Spiritualism and who is now passing through an agitated mental condition which is pulling her in two directions."

A member of the audience replied that this interpretation was accurate. She said that the brooch belonged both to her sister and herself.

The medium referred to the fact that the recipient of the message was in the habit of wearing the brooch at her waist. "When you bend down to fasten your shoes," she said, "you suddenly remember you might break it." The owner agreed that this was true. Only a week previously the thought had again struck her when she was fastening her shoes.

"This brooch has been in a drawer with a white glove laid over the top of it," said the psychometrist. "I also see on the cushion, where it has been pinned, some beaded work. Where is the little chain that used to be with it?"

"I have broken it," came the reply.

Mrs Roberts went on to say that the brooch had been lying against an ivory cross and had also been close to an old-fashioned silver locket. "My sister owns the cross, and the locket is mine," explained the owner.

"Whose strand of hair has the brooch lain against in a small box?" asked the medium. "My little niece's hair," said the owner.

Reporting her impressions upon handling a watch, Mrs Roberts stated that it had been associated with troublesome times. One of its, owners had passed over. It had been possessed first by a man, then by a woman, and lastly by another man. "It has not been worn for a considerable time," declared the medium. "I sense a wonderful character. The present owner of the watch is someone who is very patient and who, at some time, experienced two great shocks. Whose watch is this?"

"Mine," answered a member of the audience, "and all that you say is perfectly true."

"Do you know that the owner passed through a great tragedy?" asked the medium.

"Yes, I do."

"Did you know that he appeared in court where someone was fighting for life and he gave evidence which was the turning-point?"

"I know that he appeared in court."

"One owner met with a very bad accident," went on the medium. "This watch is between eighty-five and ninety years old. Do you know the young boy who now wears it?"

"I do."

"And do you know the lady who wore it on a thin chain round the neck?"

"Of course I do; I gave it to her."

"Do you know this watch has been in a folded, coloured handkerchief, close to a small clasp-knife?"

"Yes, I know that."

"What has happened to the coin that used to be attached to the watch?"

"I have it now. It is on the thin chain."

The medium then referred to the fact that, when the watch was given to the member of the audience, the glass was cracked and another one was consequently put in. Once, the watch was mislaid and was later found inside the covers of a book. "Before that," said Estelle Roberts, "it used to lie in a long square book. The book had a red cover."

"All that is perfectly true," said the person who had brought the watch.

Psychometry can be a useful form of mediumship in cases where an inquirer lives many miles away. When the inquirer sends an article used or worn by one who has died, the medium can link up the spirit owner with the one left behind on earth. This involves the addition of clairvoyance to psychometry, and disposes of that old bugbear, telepathy between medium and sitter.

It has been my rule never to deal with personal requests from correspondents who want proxy séances, but I made an exception in the case of one woman who was a complete stranger, Mrs Rachael Berry, of Owen Street, Burnley. You will see why when you read her letter:

"I am a widow at the early age of twenty-four. I have lost my dear husband after sharing together eight months of happy married life. I am absolutely desperate to hear something about him, as I am sure it would help me such a lot to bear this heavy cross. I hope you will help me, as I am so desperately lonely. If only I could talk to him, or have a message, I would be so relieved. I loved him so dearly. He died two months ago at the early age of twenty-six."

The letter, which was signed "yours in sorrow", also mentioned that the husband had used a micrometer for his work. It broke an hour before he had finished for the day. He never worked again. Moved by the writer's sorrow, I asked her to send me the micrometer, saying I would try to get a delineation from it. "This is only an experiment," I warned her, "and no results can be guaranteed." A few days later, the micrometer arrived in a parcel containing other "odds and ends", as Mrs Berry called them.

Estelle Roberts was asked whether she would psychometrise these objects. No details were provided and nothing was mentioned that would give her the slightest indication of the circumstances involved. She was merely informed that she might be able to render aid to a woman in distress. The medium psychometrised the articles and sent a detailed account of her impressions. This account was forwarded to one of my representatives, who called on Mrs Berry at her Lancashire home. It must be pointed out that Mrs Berry had not met Estelle Roberts, nor had they ever corresponded.

When my representative finished reading the medium's notes to her, Mrs Berry expressed her satisfaction. She volunteered that she and her husband had both been employed in the same factory. One day her husband said to her: "I've bad news: I've broken my `mike'." The micrometer had been in his possession ever since he started work as a young apprentice.

His wife's efforts to comfort him were not very successful. Later, he complained of a headache. At noon, his condition became so serious that a doctor was summoned. The sick man was sent to hospital, where his condition was diagnosed as cerebro-spinal fever. Three days after breaking his "mike", he passed on. The accident so worried him that even during his brief, fatal illness, he tried to repair the damaged instrument.

The moment Estelle Roberts handled the micrometer she became conscious that the dead man, whom she saw clairvoyantly, had used the instrument and that somehow it was associated with his death. "He appears to be somewhat bewildered and resentful over his passing," said the medium.

"His whole state is of one who did not wish to leave the earth, as he had so much to live for. He finds it difficult to settle down on the Other Side. He says that he has only been married a short while."

Mrs Berry had said in her letter to me that they had only been married eight months, a fact that had not, of course, been imparted to the medium.

Referring to one of the packages forwarded with the micrometer, Estelle Roberts declared that "the little box contained a carnation he had worn on his wedding day". Mrs Berry confirmed this and other facts about his passing which the medium provided.

"He keeps putting his hand to his head," stated the medium. "I also receive the impression that he was hurt before his passing." These accounts were accurate, said Mrs Berry. The fever had affected her husband's head; he constantly put his hand to his head. While he lay sick, he repeatedly fell out of his bed and his face and hands were badly bruised in consequence.

Mrs Roberts had obtained a series of names: "John, who may be called Jack, Lily or Nellie, Jim, Tom, and the initials 'R.B.'." The initials were those of the wife's name, Rachael Berry. Tom was her father's name. He and her husband were very attached to each other. Jim and Lily were friends who were looking after the dead man's dog. John was a great friend who had passed on after Berry's death and whose body lay in the grave adjoining her husband's burial place.

When my representative read the medium's words: "This young man is not yet able to register his thoughts owing to his emotion . . . his great desire was to have been left upon the earth," Mrs Berry fully understood. He had manifested far more successfully than she had expected, for he had been a Roman Catholic and opposed to Spiritualism.

Chapter 13
PERMANENT PROOFS OF SURVIVAL

FRANK LEAH is an artist for whom the dead pose in his studio. For thirty years he has used his combined talents of clairvoyance and artistry to portray thousands of dead women and children. In nearly every case, because these drawings have been identified by relatives or friends of the subjects, they provide permanent proofs of survival. He has died thousands of deaths, for inevitably he has to reproduce on himself the final earthly conditions of the people who come to life on his easel.

Leah was born with the gift of clairvoyance. As a child his psychic story follows the usual pattern—he was at first scared by the forms that he could see but which were invisible to others. He was mystified as to who these figures were, until gradually it dawned on him that they belonged to those who are dead.

For many years he was a journalist and a cartoonist, until one day he decided to combine his gifts. In the early days of his mediumship he received sitters, who always came anonymously, after they had made appointments through Spiritualist societies.

Now the usual method is for a prospective sitter to telephone him, and for Leah, if he is successful, to begin sketching a dead relative or friend of the caller, who is usually a complete stranger. While Leah sketches an outline of the spirit communicator, whom he can clairvoyantly see in his Kensington studio, he gives a running commentary of the evidence he is obtaining. Recognition is frequently complete even before the caller has seen any portrait.

The sitter is then asked to visit the artist in his studio. When he arrives he finds, in many cases, that the drawing has been completed. If it is not, the artist transforms his sketch into a portrait, making lightning alterations as he gazes at the spirit figure posing for him. Usually he asks the sitter to bring a photograph so that a comparison can be made when the drawing is finished. Sometimes Leah has foreknowledge of a telephone call. He awakens to see a spirit face in front of him. By clairaudience he is able to maintain a conversation with his visitor, glean information as to who he is and why he has returned.

The penalty of successful mediumship of the type practised by Leah is that he feels the torture of every illness, sickness and disease—all the pains from which the dead suffered before being finally freed from earth. By some magnetic link, which we do not fully understand, all spirit communicators, returning for the first time, reproduce their last earthly conditions.

They often impress on Frank Leah, for the purpose of identification, incidents connected with their lives ten, twenty, thirty or forty years ago. Occasionally these incidents are given in a wealth of detail. A woman once showed herself wearing the dress in which she was presented to Queen Victoria. Leah saw the whole court scene, thronged with its eager attendants.

Like all other mediums, he maintains that there is nothing ghostly or eerie about these spirit visitors. He does not see them as transparent phantoms. Neither do they bear any resemblance to the conventional idea of an apparition. They look solid, alive and often more vital than the people he meets in this world. He can walk round them just as if they were models posing for an artist. They will stand still while he makes a note of their shape, proportions and any other identifying characteristics. When they are strong personalities, they clearly show these characteristics, which they have temporarily reproduced, so that relatives recognise them in the medium's portraits. Leah is able to see every line and wrinkle, the colour of the eyes and hair, and to note such distinguishing features as a mole or a broken tooth. They give the kind of information about themselves, unusual names, the town or countries in which they have lived, and their professions, that produces speedy identification.

Leah is not entranced when he executes these drawings. He is quite normal. The outstanding feature is the speed with which they are done. Once he finished a complete portrait in nine seconds. Thirty seconds is fairly common when dealing with good communicators, but generally the time taken is from three to five minutes. The drawings are always lifesize. They are done in daylight in his studio.

Frequently he has made paintings from his drawings. In these the colouring, especially of the eyes, proves the reality of his clairvoyance. On many occasions he has drawn maps of foreign places he has never visited, with a detailed plan of houses and other surroundings. In a very few cases, Leah has shown his skill as a sculptor by modelling a bust of the communicator, a tribute to the detailed accuracy of his mediumship.

Leah is at pains to make it clear that he depends on the co-operation of the communicators. He cannot command them to appear. A wealthy widow, who was very anxious to have an oil painting of her deceased husband, offered him a commission of six hundred guineas. Nothing would have pleased Leah more than to accept it, but the husband refused to show himself, although he did not mind talking to the artist. Because he detested it, he had always refused to be photographed.

The artist's communicators have included people of many nationalities. Leah has a psychic drawing of a Persian Moslem, who gave his name in Persian. To show that he was a follower of Mahomet, he referred to Mecca. Further, he gave the name of a town, Kierbeleh, near Baghdad, where his body was buried. After showing himself as he usually looked, he depicted his likeness during the illness he endured before his passing, even to indicating the icebag he had on his head.

I was instrumental in being the means by which a husband and wife received great comfort when Leah drew their six-year-old child. This girl, Shirley Ann Woods, had suffered from leukaemia, a rare disease which is a kind of cancer of the blood. When she died, her parents were overwhelmed with sorrow. At my suggestion, Mrs Woods telephoned Leah without disclosing her name.

He told her at once that she sought a portrait of her child. Leah gave a perfect description of Shirley Ann, commenting on her character, appearance, hair and complexion. By the time the artist had finished, the mother was convinced that he really was looking at her daughter.

Later, when she called at his studio, she was overjoyed with the splendid likeness which he had captured. This is one of those exceptional cases where there was no comparative photograph, for the mother did not possess a picture taken at the age at which Shirley Ann showed herself to the medium. Mrs Woods asked her husband to call 'at the studio. He, too, was impressed with the drawing. In his presence, Leah did a second portrait, with added details of the daughter's appearance. In both drawings, the child was shown wearing a plaid frock. Later, Mrs Woods showed me this frock, which she had kept.

The extent of Frank Leah's successes is indicated by the fact that a book has been published on his mediumship, illustrated with some of his psychic drawings and comparative photographs of the subjects.

Despite his constant preoccupation with death, the artist's deep-throated laugh reveals his sense of humour. He says he would have preferred a monastic life. The nearest to it is the voluntary isolation that his mediumship entails. The urgings of his psychic gift, and his ability to comfort the bereaved, make the contemplative life impossible.

To replace the psychic energy utilised by his mediumship, he goes "in retreat" to a lonely estuary, where he can paint away to his heart's content. Then, refreshed, he returns to London. There he waits for the telephone bell which means that once again love is striving to bridge the chasm of death.

Chapter 14
GIFTS FROM BEYOND

I HAVE been the recipient of many gifts from the spirit world. They are known as apports (from the French, apporter, to bring). When I show my collection of apports to friends who have had no séance experience, I can sense their scepticism even when they are too polite to voice it. When courtesy is thrown to the winds and incredulity is expressed, I am not surprised.

I would find it hard to believe, had I not experienced it myself, that objects can be transported long distances, thus defying normal conceptions of time and space. But I am recording facts, and as a recorder I must be indifferent to the opinions of those who have not shared my experience. The startling fact is that some of the spirit gifts actually "grew" between my hands.

The guides of the two mediums who were responsible for bringing these apports would never take these séances seriously. It was the party spirit that animated the proceedings. Indeed, White Hawk, the guide of Mrs Kathleen Barkel, always described it as a party. It was usual to receive an invitation card, to partake of refreshments when we arrived, and to be given a present before we left.

The only physical indication that Mrs Barkel had that an apport séance would shortly take place was the curious fact that for days beforehand her figure began to swell. At the end of the séance her body resumed its normal size. I do not know the explanation. My theory is that in some way or other her body was used to store the ectoplasm required to re-materialise the objects after they had been brought through the atmosphere, doubtless in their atomic form. Obviously, with objects brought from miles away, they would first have to be dematerialised in order that the walls, bricks and mortar should prove no obstacles. The guides responsible for this phenomenon insisted that the articles were not stolen. Sometimes they were lost and could not be reclaimed because their owners had died. They might be objects that were buried beneath the earth or under the water for years, or even centuries.

Often the apport reveals careful and intelligent planning on the part of its spirit donor. The apports I have received, and that I have seen produced for others, vary in nature. Some are semi-precious stones. I have also seen a sapphire set in silver, a jade earpiece set in nine-carat gold, a gold locket and a gold ring with three opals and four diamonds.

The number of people at the séance party does not seem to affect the results. I have been present with a dozen others and as many as fifty. The number of apports received in one night has varied from twelve to twenty. The largest gifts to come were strings of mummy beads. A curious fact about Mrs Barkel's apport séances was that white light did not appear to be deleterious. When the gifts arrived, however, they had to be shielded from the light. One July evening, though the blinds were drawn, light still streamed in through the windows so that we could all see what happened quite clearly. On another occasion, the illumination was provided by a ruby lamp, sufficiently strong for me to read the notes I was making.

For the first of Mrs Barkel's apport séances I attended, I was asked by the medium's husband to examine the room.

I did so, to please my host, but it revealed nothing. White Hawk, when he controlled his medium, requested that one of the women should search her. This was done. I have always had a great affection for White Hawk, who could not be dismissed as the medium's secondary personality, for he has an individuality all his own. He is breezy and genial, with a characteristic laugh. He has wit, and his sallies reveal his humorous outlook. He always calls his medium "my coat", and the apports, no matter what their nature, were "stones". These were brought, he said, not as a scientific test, or to confound sceptics, but just to amuse his friends.

The production of the apports was a fascinating experience. The entranced Kathleen Barkel was made to stand up by White Hawk, and walk round the room with her right hand outstretched. Then he usually called one or two people to "help" him. I did so several times. I was asked to place one hand on the medium's wrist and another on her arm. In this fashion we walked round the room while White Hawk made quick grabs in space with the hand that was free. Suddenly, he would exclaim delightedly, "Got! Got!"

Then he put the medium's hands between my two hands, asking three or four people to come forward. Each had to put one hand above mine, and the other below it. This, said White Hawk, enabled the object to be restored to its original form. I was then asked to remove my hands but to keep them clasped. Presently, he asked me whether I had received my gift. "I cannot feel anything," I replied.

A few seconds later, there was a sensation of heat between the palms of my hands. Then, slowly, I felt an object becoming solid. "Hold on to it," he said. "Don't unclasp your hands." I resumed my seat, maintaining my clasped hands, noticing that the object gradually became cooler. Every few minutes, as they received their gifts, other members of the séance resumed their seats, clasping their hands. When the séance was over we were free to examine the apports. Mine, on this occasion, was an amethyst.

"How do you bring these objects here?" I asked White Hawk. He replied: "I can only explain it by telling you that I speed up the atomic vibrations until the stones are disintegrated. Then they are brought here and I slow down the vibrations until they become solid again."

On other occasions I have pressed for details of how the vibrations are speeded up and lowered. None was forthcoming. Perhaps four-dimensional happenings are beyond our three-dimensional understanding. I asked the guide to explain the stabbing motions in the air with the medium's hand. "In this work," he said, "I am helped by little spirit children, who are very mischievous. They often do not want to let the stones go. I have to distract their attention and make a grab. When I control my medium, I have left the world of four dimensions and am in three dimensions. To my helpers, it is as if I am in a cage, and so I have to cajole them." He added that the production of these apports involved having temporary control of some of the four elements—earth, fire, air and water.

One significant gift came, I was told, from Dennis Bradley, the author who was also a Bond Street tailor. I had got to know him after the tremendous furore he created with his two books describing his séance evidence. Bradley's gift arrived in similar fashion to the process I have already described. It is a small, plain, nine-carat gold ring, which presumably once belonged to the wife of a member of the Royal Air Force. Inside is engraved the motto of that service, Per ardua ad astra. This was followed by the letter "B". I regard this apport as evidence of intelligent planning. The R.A.F. motto can be translated as "Through difficulties towards the stars". Bradley's first Spiritualist book was Towards the Stars. His surname and mine both begin with "B", the letter inscribed on the ring.

Red Cloud, through Estelle Roberts, similarly treated his apport séances as parties. The last I attended was a memorable evening, for it was the successful reply to a "challenge" made by the medium's son-in-law, Kenneth Evette. A few days before, Kenneth had jokingly complained that he had never received an apport. This seemed to amuse Red Cloud, for Mrs Roberts announced that she could see her guide smiling. Red Cloud said that he would bring as a gift "anything within reason". "Could I have an apport from Egypt?" asked Evett, with a note of challenge in his voice. The medium said the guide's reply was: "Better be careful, you may get a beetle." To this Kenneth answered: "That would be fine, provided the beetle was not alive."

I was one of fifty people who assembled at this apport party, which lasted for two hours. Everyone received a gift, and some came for absent individuals. I counted them at the end of the session—there were sixty-two spirit gifts. Red Cloud's manner of production differed from that of White Hawk. The room was darkened, but a faint light came through one window. A luminous trumpet was placed in the middle of the room. Red Cloud spoke through it after his medium was entranced. Like White Hawk, he was in jocular and witty mood.

While a sitter holds the right hand of the medium, Leonard Stott, a piece of the ectoplasm, draped over his face and chest detaches itself to maintain the trumpet overhead.

A sitter is permitted to handle the ectoplasm with both his hands. Coming from the entranced medium, it forms a 'rod' to levitate the trumpet through which spirit voices were heard.

Normal photograph of Edgar Wallace.

No one has been able to produce a copy of this 'spirit' picture of Edgar Wallace. Where did it come from? It appeared, during a seance, on a plate bought by a professional photographer who loaded it into a slide, marking it as he did so. He released the camera shutter and developed the plate. The medium, John Myers, took no part in the process and merely stood in the room.

All the apports came through the trumpet, which was, as usual, a megaphone made of tin. Some were received through the narrow mouthpiece. Others came through the broad end. As the trumpet gyrated and whirled above our heads, we could often hear the objects rattling inside as they presumably became solidified. One extraordinary fact was that some of the gifts which came through the mouthpiece were larger than its diameter, as I proved by measuring them. Like White Hawk, Red Cloud would delightedly say, "Got!" This indicated that a gift was ready for presentation. The guide named the individual who was to come forward and receive it. You placed your hands beneath the trumpet and heard it rattle through until it dropped into your palms.

The party spirit was in evidence from the start. Charles, the medium's husband, was proud of his collection of apports. He kept some of them in a wash-leather receptacle, in a wallet, which reposed in a buttoned-up pocket specially made on the inside of his waistcoat.

"Have you got all your apports?" Red Cloud asked him. "Yes," he replied, tapping the slight bulge he could feel when he touched his jacket. "Here are two that you haven't got," said the guide. "Come forward." Charles moved to the trumpet, heard the familiar rattling sound and received once again the two apports that were deposited on his person when the séance began.

Meanwhile, as apport after apport was received, Kenneth Evett waited impatiently. After about an hour, a curious splashing sound, reminiscent of waves breaking, could be heard within the trumpet. Then Red Cloud asked Iris Evett, Kenneth's wife, to approach the trumpet and receive for her husband "one of the most sacred beetles, a most beautiful specimen". The guide asked that it be handled carefully and not pressed too hard, as it was not yet sufficiently solidified.

My curiosity aroused, I asked Red Cloud where the apport had come from. "Abydos," he replied. As I had never heard this name before, I inquired if Red Cloud would kindly spell it. He did so, letter by letter, while I recorded the name.

The climax to the séance was the production of about a dozen apports, pouring through the trumpet at the same moment. Later, I examined the scarab with interest. It was a beautiful specimen, and edged with gold. Other gifts received that night included two figures of Buddha, some praying beads, and a collection of precious and semi-precious stones, sapphires, emeralds, rubies, amethysts, turquoise, onyx, topaz and opals.

Kenneth Evett provided a fitting sequel when I next met him. His curiosity aroused, he had gone to the British Museum, to the Department of Egyptian Antiquities. There he had produced his apport, and asked for an expert opinion. He was told that it was genuine, a fine specimen, of the type usually found in . . . Abydos!

* * *

Sir Arthur Conan Doyle was responsible for an apport which made a tremendous impression on his family. The medium, Mrs Caird Miller, discovered her psychic powers in extraordinary circumstances. She is a woman of culture and marked intelligence, a Scot with all the qualities of caution associated with that race.

Mrs Caird Miller knew practically nothing of Spiritualism until a series of strange events happened shortly after Sir

Arthur's passing. In parenthesis, I would mention that while her mediumship functioned she was the head of a commercial undertaking and found her business acumen was in no way impaired.

Although a widow twice bereaved, Mrs Caird Miller had no interest in psychic matters until she had a curious conversation with a stranger. Seated in the tea-room of a large West End store, she noticed that a woman at her table seemed anxious to get into conversation with her. Her natural reserve made her resent this approach from a stranger, but the woman was insistent. "I am a Spiritualist," she said, "and I saw you in a vision this morning."

This comment annoyed Mrs Caird Miller, who regarded the stranger as a crank. Nothing, however, would daunt the woman, who proceeded to describe a spirit form that she said was visible to her in the tea-room. This made Mrs Caird Miller take notice, for it was a perfect description of her husband, who had died not long before.

Her curiosity aroused, she made an extensive inquiry into Spiritualism, finally discovering that she herself possessed a psychic gift. Unmistakable voices would speak to her and give definite messages. Often these voices gave information on matters unknown to her, but which, on inquiry, she always found were correct.

About a month after Conan Doyle's death, she heard a voice declare in clear tones: "I am Arthur Conan Doyle. I want you to get into touch with my wife and send her a message."

This surprised Mrs Caird Miller, who had never met the great writer. She did not know his wife or any member of his family. Her reserve was a barrier to approaching Lady

Doyle unless she were absolutely sure of her ground. "Give me some proof of your identity," she demanded. The voice replied by giving the initials of every member of his family. When she made inquiries she found that they were all accurate.

Still hesitant, she said to the Doyle voice when it next repeated the request: "Where shall I find your wife?" The reply came quite clearly. The voice gave her a telephone number, told her she would not find it in the telephone book, but said it was the unlisted number of the Doyle cottage in the New Forest.

This was a test. Still cautious, Mrs Caird Miller decided that before approaching Lady Doyle she would try to ascertain whether the number was correct. She inquired of the telephone exchange, but was met with the reply that they were not allowed to divulge such information.

Here was a deadlock. Mrs Caird Miller hesitated for a few moments and then asked the operator to call the number the voice had given her. The number was accurate, for soon she was talking to Lady Doyle. At that time the Doyle family were being flooded with alleged spirit messages from all over the world. Lady Doyle and her two sons rightly insisted that they would not accept spirit communications claiming to emanate from Sir Arthur unless they were accompanied by irrefutable evidence to prove their authenticity.

This was indeed a rebuff. Mrs Caird Miller had carried out the instructions of the voice, and had met with failure. She determined to have nothing more to do with it. But Sir Arthur was undismayed. A few days later she heard his voice again. He knew all about the rebuff, he said, but he was determined to prove himself through this new medium.

"Will you go and have a séance with Mrs Deane?" he asked, "and I will appear on a photograph."

This sitting with Mrs Deane, a medium for spirit photography, was arranged anonymously, and no hint was given of its purpose. When the plate was developed and a print made, in addition to Mrs Caird Miller's photograph there was a striking "extra" of Conan Doyle above her head. This spirit "extra" was shown to Lady Doyle, who admitted that it was a remarkable one which bore an unquestionable resemblance to her husband. Even then, however, she demanded still more proof.

That, thought Mrs Caird Miller, was the last straw. But the persistent Conan Doyle provided the required proof. It came a few days later, when Mrs Caird Miller was in her London flat. She had not long awakened and had gone into another room. When she returned to her bedroom, she found a key lying on her pillow. She looked at the key in amazement. It did not belong to any door in her flat. How it got there was a mystery.

As she stood there, wondering, she heard the now familiar Conan Doyle voice say: "That is my key. It comes from the door of my study, which is always kept closed, at Crowborough. Send for my son, Denis." Here was a test—if the statement were true.

Mrs Caird Miller telephoned Denis Conan Doyle at Crowborough, Sussex, and told him what had happened. In a few minutes he had jumped into a motor car and was on his way to London. He arrived at Mrs Caird Miller's flat, and took the key back to Crowborough. Later he telephoned to say that it was certainly the key of his father's study. Sir Arthur had transported it a distance of forty miles. That convinced Lady Doyle.

Thereafter, Mrs Caird Miller became the medium through whom spirit messages were regularly transmitted from Sir Arthur to his wife and family.

Chapter 15
EDGAR WALLACE COMES BACK

SPIRIT photography, when it is successful, provides among the best examples of permanent evidence for life after death. When you receive a photograph of one you love, and are satisfied beyond doubt that the production of this spirit extra cannot be explained by trickery, then you have a greatly treasured memento. I do not blame sceptics for assuming that fraud must be the explanation. The production of these extras is so remarkable a happening that you require incontrovertible evidence before being convinced that the face of the dead relative or friend has been placed on the plate by spirit power.

Fraud, however, entails the use of a highly complex organisation that could not be kept secret. The medium, or an accomplice, must know in advance who is coming for a séance. Somehow or other there must be access to old family albums, with photographs being removed for copying without this fact being discovered. Alternatively, the medium, or a confederate, must learn beforehand the town where the deceased person lived, and conduct a search among its photographers, looking for pictures taken anything from twenty to fifty years ago.

If these were the methods by which spirit photographers worked they would soon be exposed. You cannot break into houses and steal pictures from albums without being found out. Neither can you conduct long and exhaustive inquiries among photographers without arousing suspicion. When a news story breaks and an unknown person suddenly achieves prominence, there is a feverish hunt by reporters among the relatives and photographers in the vicinity, but obviously it is soon known for what they are looking.

John Myers was a dentist in Victoria when his interest in Spiritualism was aroused by a medium telling him that he possessed the gift of psychic photography. With a few friends and some sympathetic Spiritualists, he formed a circle to cultivate his gift, with speedy and startling results. His wife, however, was not altogether pleased with this development. Like her husband, she belonged to the Jewish faith, but being the daughter of a rabbi she was far more orthodox than her partner. The first time I met her, she earnestly consulted me as to whether it was right, from a religious viewpoint, for a Jew to be a medium.

After conducting my own stringent test, I was satisfied with the genuineness of John Myers's mediumship. In a later test Edgar Wallace was involved in a series of happenings that were more fantastic than any plot that his ingenious mind had devised on earth. Though dead, the master craftsman of thrilling fiction excelled himself with an afterlife drama.

His story began with my receiving a parcel containing what was alleged to be automatic writing from a woman in South Wales. In her accompanying letter she stated in handwriting, far from literate, that the manuscript contained communications from Edgar Wallace describing his life from the moment of his passing. I noticed that the preface had a foreword dedicated, "To my old friend Hannen Swaffer."

As I was almost late for an appointment with the famous

journalist, I parcelled the manuscript without reading it and took it with me. When I arrived in Swaffer's flat I produced it for his inspection. I expected this hard-bitten, cynical journalist to dismiss the manuscript and was intrigued to see that he went on reading it for quite a long time. Finally he observed: "I cannot say whether it was written by Edgar Wallace, but it certainly emanates from a trained reporter and observer."

Here was a dilemma. If the automatic writing were genuine, its publication would arouse tremendous interest. I followed a plan which will surprise non-Spiritualists. At the next voice séance with Estelle Roberts, I explained my problem to Red Cloud and asked if he could help me. "Don't do anything about the manuscript until I have spoken to Wallace," the guide replied. A fortnight later, Red Cloud announced that he had spoken to Wallace, who said that he was the author of this automatic-writing script.

I published it, in weekly instalments, under the title "My Life After Death—by Edgar Wallace", and it created a furore. Members of his family were not pleased with its publication. Bob Curtis, who had been Wallace's secretary, was vehement in denouncing it as bearing no resemblance to his former employer's style.

In the midst of all this raging excitement, I engaged a new reporter. I had telephoned the National Union of Journalists and asked that the next reporter who called looking for a post should be sent to me. Along came a young man named A. W. Austen. He was frank in acknowledging his scepticism about Spiritualism, and stated that he was an agnostic about religion.

The total extent of his experience of Spiritualism had been

to attend one or two meetings when he was a reporter on a local North London newspaper. I engaged him, saying that all I wanted was that he should report fairly what he heard at séances and Spiritualist gatherings.

A test séance with John Myers was his first assignment. I asked Austen to lay down the conditions that he would regard as proving Myers's mediumship, and all these were accepted. Austen himself bought the plates in a shop of his own choosing, marked them so as to make substitution impossible, loaded them into slides and later into the camera.

Myers did not handle any part of the photographic process. All he did was to be present in the room when the pictures were taken. The medium, who is also clairvoyant, described the spirit presence of Israel Zangwill, the well-known Jewish novelist. When the plates were developed and prints made, one contained an extra of Zangwill.

The sequel to its publication was a letter from a Fleet Street photographic agency asking for a reproduction fee. They claimed that while the extra was not an exact copy, it resembled their copyright photograph of this novelist.

I explained to two representatives of the agency who called on me that the Zangwill extra was obtained under test conditions. Any payment of a reproduction fee might imply that this result had been fraudulently obtained. As they were obviously sceptical about spirit photography, I invited them to conduct their own test of John Myers. These highly professional photographers were more than willing to have this experience. The conditions, to which the medium readily agreed, were arranged.

They would buy the plates in a shop of their choice, initial them as they were loaded into the slides, place them in the camera, be present when the exposures were made, and take charge of the developing and fixing. Myers was not to touch any of the material used. His part would be to say when the exposures should be made.

The agreed procedure was followed. Unknown to us at the time, however, the representative, who was to initial the plates when loading them into slides, used a sharp-pointed instrument to cut them so that this mark and his initials could later be identified. Neither the medium nor I was told about this extra precaution.

While the photographs were being taken, Myers announced that clairvoyantly he could see Edgar Wallace in the room. He transmitted this message from Wallace, which had a bearing on the Zangwill extra: "If any picture does come, it will be unlike any in existence."

When the plates were developed and contact prints made, on one of them there was almost a perfect likeness of Edgar Wallace. No one has ever produced a copy. If the genuineness of this result is to be doubted, the question for sceptics to answer is: How can a medium produce an identifiable photograph of Edgar Wallace when there is no duplicate to be found anywhere in the world?

In a signed statement, the representatives of the photographic agency agreed that the test conditions had been fulfilled and volunteered: "There was no substitution of plates." The negative containing the Wallace spirit extra clearly showed the initials and the secret mark made at the time it was placed into its slide.

Very often in Spiritualism, the evidence received can be compared with the pieces of a jig-saw puzzle. The Wallace extra is a case in point. A few days later, at an Estelle Roberts voice séance, Red Cloud surprised me by requesting that I pick up the trumpets and hold them. When I asked the reason for doing so, he said that Edgar Wallace was present and was trying to communicate. As he was not familiar with the technique and had not consulted Red Cloud, the guide had to restrain him because of damage that might ensue to the medium.

At the next voice séance, Wallace himself spoke, and proved to be a first-class communicator. He confirmed, if confirmation were necessary, that he had been present at the John Myers séance and had succeeded in transmitting his likeness on to the plate. He also confirmed that he was responsible for the automatic-writing script I had published. Told about his secretary's disclaimer, Wallace replied: "Tell Bob Curtis not to be a fool." He promised to give Curtis something that would cause him furiously to think.

A few weeks later, Curtis had an astonishing story to tell. After being Wallace's secretary for fifteen years, he had now begun to act in a similar capacity to Sydney Horler, also famous as a thriller writer. Horler had sent Curtis some dictaphone records of his next novel to be transcribed. Curtis placed the first dictaphone record on to a cylinder and "was startled almost out of my seat to hear the unmistakable voice of Edgar Wallace coming through". This voice said: "I use this to dictate my books—my stories."

How did Wallace's voice get on to the dictaphone record? The mystery proved insoluble so far as normal explanations are concerned. One suggestion was that Wallace had possibly used the record, and it had been imperfectly shaved and re-polished. That explanation did not fit, for Horler's voice would have been superimposed on Wallace's and the two would have been blurred. As it was, they were quite distinct, with Horler's voice coming after that of Edgar's.

The mysterious record was taken to the Dictaphone offices, where the position was explained to one of their experts. He played the record back and heard Wallace's voice. This was followed by Horler's voice in deeper tones, saying: "It was not until an early hour in the morning that Brendle had . . ." the opening words of Horler's story.

Curtis could not be moved in his declaration that the first voice belonged to Wallace. The record was examined under a powerful magnifying glass. The expert found that there was no break between the point where the first voice ended and the second one began. "It is a hundred to one against two people being able to speak on the same record without showing a break where the needle records on the wax," he said.

To discount any theory of incomplete shaving, the expert partly shaved a used record and then showed the result. Where the shaving left off, there was a slight but distinct ridge. The mystery record had no such ridge. Edgar Wallace had fulfilled his spirit promise. As he later said at another voice séance: "I have given old Bob something to think about."

Months afterwards, when I had forgotten about these happenings, I was attending my usual voice séance with Estelle Roberts. Red Cloud surprised me by saying: "I have been to see Mrs Hopkins at Porthcawl."

"Why?" I asked. With a chuckle, the guide answered: "To see if she has received any more writing from Edgar Wallace." When I published "My Life After Death—by Edgar Wallace," I had deliberately refrained from giving either the medium's name, or that of the town in which she lived, so that she should not be bombarded by reporters. Red Cloud, by showing that he knew them both, had provided the fitting sequel to the Edgar Wallace spirit drama.

These flash-light pictures taken in the Glen Hamilton seance room show five miniature materialisations. They are all the faces of the Rev. C. H. Spurgeon, the famous preacher. Alongside are the nearest comparable earthly photographs. Note that the miniature face C' is not fully formed due to a misunderstanding about the signal for the photograph; the ectoplasm which was receding into the medium's head is in a state of partial disintegration.

Chapter 16
THEY CURE "INCURABLES"

THE acid test of spirit healing is that it must achieve permanent cures after all other means have failed. Hundreds of such cases can be produced. Mrs Peggy Parish, of Christchurch Road, East Sheen, London, was cured of cancer after the medical verdict was that she had only six months to live. That was nearly thirty years ago. There is no doubt about the diagnosis, because it was confirmed by a pathological test.

Mrs Parish had already undergone one operation in a nursing home. A second operation was advised because the laboratory test had proved the serious nature of the malignant growth. She came home to prepare for the ordeal.

Meanwhile, her husband was told by a medium, at a time when he was unsympathetic to Spiritualism, that he possessed healing power which could cure his wife. The only indication of this power, if such it were, had been that when he visited his wife in the nursing home, she always said she felt better for his presence. He assumed that the reason may have been a psychological one.

Naturally he asked the medium how he could cure his wife. He was given precise instructions that involved laying-on of hands. This proved so successful that the second operation became unnecessary. It has never taken place.

Inspired by this remarkable happening, the husband retired from a lucrative post and dedicated his whole life to healing the sick. He has since passed on to that larger life which inspired him. But his wife, who is a living miracle, continues the work of healing in the sanctuary that was built for her husband.

Spirit healing is among the most beneficent activities performed in Spiritualism. The healer is a medium who acts as a channel for a higher power that is directed by intelligent beings in the Beyond. In the ultimate, of course, all healing, whether termed spirit, spiritual, faith, psychic or divine, stems from one source. It is not part of my function to decry healing achieved in other spheres by other methods. An infinite God can be reached in an infinite number of ways. None can have a monopoly of infinite power. Neither can divine forces be commanded as to where they shall operate.

Every kind of spiritual healing is dependent on a process of attunement achieved by the human instrument. Where mediumship is concerned, this is a conscious co-operation with spirit guides. Our evidence is that some of them were distinguished in the medical world when on earth, have added to their knowledge since passing, and voluntarily return to heal the afflicted.

Spirit healing is directed towards treating the cause of the disease, as distinct from the effect. It is the considered view of modern doctors that the majority of diseases originate in the mind. A simple illustration is that ulcers are caused by worry. Tension, fear, frustration, rage, envy, hatred—all these produce physical reactions. Obviously, in these psychosomatic diseases, as they are called, treating the symptoms or effects does not achieve a cure. If you remove the ulcers and the patient goes on worrying, he will get more ulcers,

Healing mediums are channels for a dynamic spirit power

that either stimulates the body's natural self-recuperative processes, or brings the equivalent of the life force to remove the cause of the disease. The body is a self-healing organism, but disease prevents its innate curative processes from fulfilling their function.

Mediums like Harry Edwards are erroneously described as "faith healers". There is undoubtedly some help if the patient has faith in the healer. The overwhelming majority of patients treated by Edwards, whose postbag is frequently two thousand letters a day, receive absent healing because they live at a distance. Many of them are separated from the healer by oceans and continents. Of these absent healing treatments, a large proportion is given to sufferers who do not know that application has been made by relatives and friends on their behalf. As they are unaware of receiving treatment at a distance, there cannot be any faith on their part. Neither can there be any faith in the minds of thousands of young children whom Edwards heals.

The statistics he has compiled show that improvement is achieved with eighty per cent. of his patients and cures with thirty per cent. These are surprising figures when you realise that few people venture to consult a spirit healer except as a last resort.

These triumphs of healing, especially those performed at a distance, imply a highly organised spirit campaign. In some manner, every person who writes to the healer makes a psychic link which enables the sufferer to receive treatment. Put this way it does not sound any more remarkable than radar, radio or television. We accept these marvels because they are now commonplace, but if anyone had foretold them a century ago he would have been regarded as a lunatic. It seems to me no more difficult to believe that spirit power can reach those with whom it has made a psychic link than that a radio wave can travel round the earth quicker than sound can cross a room.

Edwards is conscious of having travelled, in his astral body, to some of his patients, for he has been able to describe the surroundings and details of the rooms he has visited. Many of the sufferers claim to have seen his astral body, or even the forms of spirit operators, who are part of the healing band in the Beyond.

Apart from possessing the healing gift, Edwards maintains that this type of medium must have compassion, a love of humanity and an overwhelming desire to remove the burden from the afflicted. In Edwards's case, as with most mediums, he has learned about suffering at first hand, so that sympathy for fellow-sufferers came naturally. He endured hardship and poverty for many years. When he married he was so poor that he had to borrow money for the wedding ring. The bailiff, who frequently called with court orders, when Edwards was troubled with business worries, soon became a personal friend.

The healer, too, must have the patience of Job, for every sufferer yearns to describe all his ailments in detail. Though he has listened to thousands of catalogues of pains and aches, Edwards never loses his sympathetic approach. He has the great gift of devoting all his attention to the sufferer who is being treated.

Thousands have seen Edwards demonstrate healing at the largest halls in their own cities and towns. They have watched him perform the "impossible". It is not done by manipulation as used by osteopaths and chiropractors.

Edwards has had no lessons in the art of manipulation, yet he frees locked limbs with a dexterity that has to be seen to be believed—and it is all done without causing pain.

When Edwards began his healing mission he knew virtually nothing about the body and its mechanism. So ignorant was he about the majority of diseases that he had to consult a medical dictionary to find out the meaning of the complaints mentioned by sufferers. Today I am sure he would qualify as an expert on the human body, its construction, mechanism, functioning and all the diseases that beset it.

Years of attunement with the spirit power which flows through him have taught Edwards exactly what to do in every situation. He waits for the moment when he knows he must perform the healing, which is always done with his eyes closed. When this moment comes, Edwards frees a rigid limb, straightens a curved spine, or will "pull" a shortened leg until it is as long as its companion.

It has been said that his results are due to suggestion, hysteria or even mass-hypnotism. These nonsensical suggestions could come only from critics who have not seen Edwards at work. At all his public demonstrations there is no attempt to induce religious fervour, hysteria or emotionalism. No lights are lowered or spotlights used.

Naturally he has to confine himself to ailments where the audience can see the benefit of treatment. How could he show that an ulcer had vanished? He always welcomes the co-operation of medical men, both before and after treatment. They are asked, for example, to check the extent of a spinal curvature before treatment and to announce the result after the healing has been given. I have never heard one doctor assert that the healing has been a failure.

Though officially Medicine does not recognise that spirit healing is responsible for curing "incurables", hundreds of doctors have applied, and still do, to Edwards for treatment. Their applications are made for relatives, friends, patients, and even for themselves. I have read their letters in which they frankly express astonishment at the successes achieved in cases where they knew they could do no more. Medical etiquette forbids them being named, but the recipients of spirit healing include even distinguished specialists and surgeons. They have taken a risk in co-operating with Edwards, because disciplinary action has been threatened by the British Medical Association. Indeed, they have warned that such doctors may be struck off the medical register.

Six members of our royal family have been treated by Edwards, a fact which has not helped official Medicine to view this "unregistered practitioner" with favour. After all, the royal family has the highest medical skill at its disposal.

When Edwards treats a patient he usually receives an "inward diagnosis" as to the cause of the trouble and an indication where healing power is to be applied. If a patient has a leg ailment, Edwards "knows" whether the cause lies in the leg, or in the spine, or head, or wherever it may be. As soon as his fingers touch the seat of the trouble the healing power flows through. No force is ever needed. When the healing is over, Edwards experiences a sense of happiness that "the work has been done". At first, he had to learn to trust this "inner knowledge", for sometimes he could not believe that the treatment had been given and success achieved.

The medium, Jack Webber, is lashed to his chair so that he cannot free himself. Black cotton has been threaded around a button on his jacket, through a button hole, and then knotted. Normally the cotton would snap if the coat were removed.

Eight seconds later the medium's coat has been completely removed but knots and ropes are undisturbed though roping is a little looser because the jacket has been removed.

(See next page)

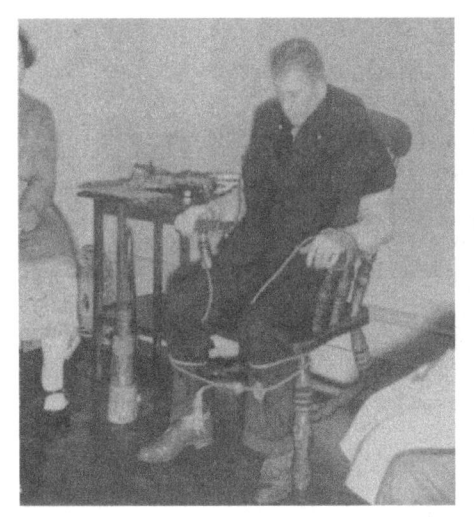

Ten seconds later. The coat is seen in the process of returning. It is halfway on the medium's body, The sleeves partially back in their original position. The front of the coat is semi-transparent. Waistcoat buttons are visible through it.

Fourteen seconds later. The jacket is now completely restored to its former position. All the ropes, knots and black cotton thread are intact and in original positions. Between the taking of these infra-red pictures the medium's guide asked for the white light to be put on so that Webber could be seen with his coat removed.

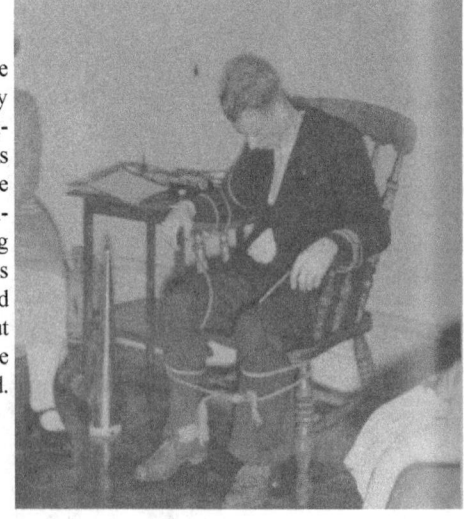

He seldom feels fatigue, even though a demonstration may last for an hour and a half. Often, he avers, he feels fresher afterwards than he did before. His sensations during healing he describes as those of exquisite pleasure and sheer delight, greater than any physical exaltation.

Edwards has to avoid making up his mind as to what can or cannot be done. Once there came a blind patient. The eyes appeared to be disintegrated. There was no iris, nor was there a pupil, only a smeary mess of streaks. Edwards's own verdict of healing in this case was, "Not possible". Then he felt the healing power flow through him. In a few minutes the eyes, sightless from birth, could see shades of light. Later the patient said that she could see colour. Three months afterwards, while seated in a moving train, the patient could see the telegraph poles.

I can name one doctor who co-operated with Edwards. As she has died there is no danger of her being "struck off". She was Dr Margaret Vivian, who for many years ran a successful nursing home at Southbourne, Hants. At my suggestion she asked Edwards to give absent healing to four patients whom she and other doctors could not cure. The sufferers were not told about the experiment.

The first was a victim of sycosis barbae, a distressing skin disease. For nearly two years he had received expert treatment from the skin departments of hospitals in London and the provinces. Though temporary improvement was occasionally observed, the sores on his face did not heal. The area they covered slowly increased. From the time when absent healing began, improvement was gradual, until finally the face was entirely healed.

Case number two was a woman suffering from a steady

deterioration in health for which no adequate cause could be found. Her condition worsened until she could scarcely walk and found it difficult to force herself to eat. It was late autumn when Edwards was asked to give absent healing. For some weeks there was no particular improvement. Then suddenly, on Christmas Day, she felt better and, to her friends' surprise, ate a large dinner of turkey and plum pudding. She improved steadily. When Dr Vivian examined her, she found her "in excellent health".

The third patient suffered from a stubborn varicose ulcer on the skin, complicated by varicose veins of long standing. Once again there was no visible improvement for the first few months. Then followed a rapid healing.

The last patient was a woman who had suffered for years from varicose veins. "Both legs were much swollen," said Dr Vivian. "The least abrasion threatened an indolent ulcer similar to that of case number three." Distant healing first reduced the swelling, then achieved a cure, the patient herself declaring that she felt ten years younger.

Edwards has tried to interest the Church of England, but officially it will have nothing to do with him. The cures of "incurables" he submitted, by invitation, to its last commission were suppressed in its report. Nevertheless large numbers of clergymen consult him. Edwards has conducted a joint healing service with a vicar in front of the altar in an Anglican church at Hove, Sussex. He has demonstrated healing in more than one Congregationalist church, and has helped to train one of its ministers who had the healing gift. This minister has trained other colleagues who had the latent healing ability.

Edwards recognises, as a fundamentally religious man,

that healing should be performed in all places of worship, and especially in those churches which claim to owe allegiance to One who said: "Heal the sick." You cannot, however, co-operate with doctors or clergymen who do not wish to co-operate with you. Edwards is neither a medical man nor a cleric. Nevertheless, he is a great healer, endowed with the divine gift.

It is by utilising this gift as an instrument, claiming no credit for himself, that he performs what are called "miracles of healing". You can put it another way and say that he is one of the means by which sufferers have a second chance, access to a higher tribunal after the dreaded word "incurable" has been pronounced in their cases.

* * *

One of the great difficulties that doctors have in accepting spirit healing is that it breaks all the rules laid down in the text-books they studied in medical colleges. It does not seem to help to point out that nearly every outstanding advance in medicine has had to face the opposition of those with orthodox outlooks. Non-medical pioneers met with even greater hostility to their therapies.

Sir Herbert Barker, denounced as a "quack", lived long enough to wear down the enmity to his bone-setting manipulations, and finally was invited to teach his methods to doctors. Freud aroused a storm with his psycho-analysis, which is now medically respectable as psychiatry. Mesmerism was "fraudulent", but hypnotism, which is its child, is regularly employed in Harley Street.

Today there is at least one specialist in what A. J. Cronin

called "The Citadel", who offers his patients a choice of orthodox treatment or spiritual healing. They can have either all the skill which this specialist has shown in treating famous athletes or, in the same consulting rooms, they can go into the one furnished as a sanctuary, where, with equal sincerity, he offers the spiritual healing which has performed many "miracles".

Tell a medical man that spirit healing has cured an incurable disease and his reaction is, not surprisingly, one of scepticism. He has been trained to believe that there are certain prescribed treatments for all known diseases. Incidentally, history shows that there are fashions in treatments—leeches, blood-letting, removing the appendix and now antibiotics. If the greatest medical skill cannot obtain a cure, why should a doctor believe that an unregistered practitioner, with no medical training, without having studied physiology, and often not even knowing the right names for diseases, should succeed? "No," he argues, "there must be a mistake. Perhaps the patient was wrongly diagnosed."

Told that the diagnosis is confirmed by X-ray plates, the excuse is sometimes offered that the plates must have got confused with those belonging to another patient. Another alternative, he will tell you, is that sometimes there are spontaneous recoveries and natural remissions.

It is exceedingly difficult to get any specialist to certify that a patient was suffering from an incurable disease and that he has been cured of it. In a long experience I have known of only two specialists who provided such written testimony in connection with successful treatment for malignant growths. One specialist marked his document, "Private and confidential". The other headed his certificate,

"Confidential and private".

The final medical argument offered is that the healing has not effected a cure but only a temporary alleviation. This raises the question of how permanent is "permanent"? The answer is to produce the evidence. I have already mentioned the photographic mediumship of John Myers, who also possesses the healing gift to a very marked degree.

It is now twenty-six years since I met Laurence Parish, a New York businessman with an international reputation. One reason for his visit to London was to consult specialists concerning his sciatica of ten years standing, and his eyesight, which had been defective since childhood. For his sciatica he had consulted the leading authorities in more than one capital. Being a wealthy man, he had spent vast sums on the most modern appliances, and in trying every known remedy, without obtaining any relief. His sight was so poor that twelve months previously, when he had changed his spectacles, he was told that within the next year or two he would have to wear bi-focal lenses of the greatest strength that could be made.

Parish was so intrigued and sceptical about Myers's spirit photography that he asked me to introduce him to the medium, as he would like to experiment for himself. Myers agreed to the most rigid tests that Parish could devise. This involved the purchase of everything in connection with the photographic process, from the camera to the dish in which the plates were developed. He had part of his Savoy Hotel suite transformed into a dark room. Myers was not allowed to touch anything connected with the photographic tests. The results obtained dumbfounded Parish, and convinced him that he was confronted with a power that did not emanate from this world. On the plates he saw faces of dead people he could recognise, whose bodies had been buried on the other side of the Atlantic Ocean. Yet Myers was a complete stranger and had never visited America.

At the end of the second day of his experiments, Parish asked the medium a simple question. Seeing that he possessed a power by means of which spirit extras appeared on plates, could it be used to heal him? Myers, who saw that Parish was in great pain, answered that this was a matter with which only his spirit guide could deal. Parish persisted and said he would like, if possible, to consult the guide. There and then, Myers was entranced, and the question was addressed to his guide.

This invisible figure, speaking through the medium's lips, made the astonishing statement that on the following morning, when Parish awoke, he would find that he was cured of his sciatica. A surprised Laurence Parish had only a few hours to test this assertion, which proved accurate when he awoke the next day. For the first time for years he felt no pain and was able to walk normally. In great excitement, he called Myers to tell him the joyful news. To prove the cure was complete, he discarded the specially thick underwear which it had been essential for him to wear.

This remarkable overnight cure emboldened him to make one further request. It would be still greater testimony to spirit healing, he said, if he could return to New York and appear among his friends without wearing spectacles. Myers's reply was similar—his guide must be consulted. This time Parish was told that the defective sight would be cured, but it would take a few days. A week later, Parish telephoned Myers early in the morning to say that he was about to call on him. The second miracle had been achieved. He could see without his glasses. Before leaving London for New York, he destroyed his spectacles. His own testimony was: "I can now read without my glasses a newspaper or any other printed matter with more facility than I could have done previously by using them."

Parish, a cautious businessman, decided to consult his specialists again. He offered himself for re-examination to the medical experts in London who had been unable to afford him relief for his sciatica. When the examination was completed, with the verdict that there was no sign of this ailment, Parish was asked what had happened. He decided it would be profitless to give the reason. A similar scene was re-enacted when he visited the eye specialist.

Up to the time of my writing these words, twenty-six years later, Parish has had no return of his sciatica, or of his defective sight. The cures have been maintained. Are twenty-six years "permanent"?

Parish invited Myers to join his American commercial concern, which has international ramifications. Myers at the time was a dentist, practising his mediumship with no thought of a commercial career. He had never crossed the Channel, and was not enamoured of the idea of sailing the Atlantic Ocean, but finally he accepted. Today, if you wanted to see him, you would find him in a typically successful American businessman's office in the skyscraper known as Rockefeller Plaza, where he is vice-president of the company.

This is a story which proves that "truth is stranger than fiction", which, after all, as someone said, is only another way of saying that the works of God exceed the works of man.

Chapter 17
DEAD DOCTOR DIAGNOSES

FOR over thirty years Scottish specialists and doctors have regularly consulted a Glasgow housewife because of her skilful diagnoses. She is Margaret Lyon, who has been called, "The woman who can X-ray with her eyes closed". The diagnostic talent does not belong to Mrs Lyon but to the dead Japanese woman doctor who works through her in trance.

Margaret Lyon's mediumship is also responsible for the fact that there are nearly a hundred Church of Scotland ministers practising spiritual healing. She helped to develop the healing gift that was latent in their ministerial pioneer. He in turn helped to unfold a similar talent in other mini-sters. Even today most of them do not know that it all began with a healing medium.

In thirty years Margaret Lyon cannot recall one case in which her trance diagnoses have proved inaccurate, even though occasionally they have flatly contradicted medical opinion. You can imagine the kind of situation that has arisen when some of her patients have been medical men who knew that the diagnoses they had received were the most expert available to them. To these arguments there is always one reply. The medium asserts that a test on guinea-pigs, or with the patient's blood, or X-ray plates, will prove her right.

Thus it is not surprising to learn that sufferers who become her patients—there is a very long waiting list—are never asked for a recital of their troubles. They are told in detail what is wrong with them. The cause of the malady is often traced to an incident in the past which has sometimes been forgotten.

It was personal suffering that originally brought Margaret Lyon into the healing domain. Her son, barely two years of age, suffered from a mysterious disease which no doctor or specialist could diagnose. When the mother had reached the depths of despair, a friend suggested she should try spirit healing. Mrs Lyon was recommended to visit Govan, where a Clyde shipwright, a medium named Jerry Nicholson, practised this form of mediumship.

As a last resort, the mother called with her boy. The entranced healer, without asking any questions, immediately examined the child's head. Soon he diagnosed the cause of the trouble as a milk worm which had attacked the brain, and expressed his regret that it was too late for any recovery to be made.

On the following day, the boy lapsed into a coma. He was taken to hospital, where he stayed for three weeks and then died. A post-mortem examination produced the verdict, "Death from bovine meningitis." The medium had been proved right.

This experience made her realise what spirit healing could achieve if it could be applied to sufferers in time. She prayed that she could be used in some way to help other mothers who might be placed in a plight similar to her own. When a medium later told her that she possessed the healing gift in embryonic form, Margaret Lyon determined to unfold it.

For two years she was an assiduous member of a developing circle which met once a week. Because nothing happened, she decided reluctantly that perhaps, after all, she was not intended to be a healer. Then came what she decided must be her last séance. All that she remembers is that she fell asleep. Apologising, when she awoke, for what she thought was a breach of good manners, she was surprised to be told that she had not been asleep. Instead, someone who claimed to be a spirit Japanese woman doctor had spoken through her.

The visitor from another world had given the name of Kahesdee, which, translated, meant, "I serve". Kahesdee had announced that, with the co-operation of her medium, a great service could be rendered to the suffering, and that she would specialise in the treatment of tuberculosis, a significant statement in view of the fact that this disease had been responsible for the death of Mrs Lyon's child.

Throughout the years, Kahesdee has shown that she possesses a wide range of medical knowledge, is familiar with the technical phraseology employed by doctors, and conversant with the latest researches in therapeutics. She speaks softly and works with a competence that is highly impressive to watch. Her sense of humour is of the quiet variety, and she chats merrily all the time she gives treatment. Typical of her humour is the aside she once made to me: "I expect I'm the chattiest ghost you have ever met."

Many observers have commented on the fact that when Mrs Lyon is entranced her face, eyes and bodily posture all suggest the Oriental. Kahesdee has given me some details about her earthly life.

"I was taught by a Japanese priest who had been to Stoneyhurst College," she said. She was a doctor attached to the royal household at Korea in 1895, at the time when it was attacked by the Japanese. The invaders burned and buried alive the Queen and all members of the royal household. Kahesdee says that she died as a result of exposure at the early age of twenty-three.

The Queen had been anxious to introduce new ideas on hygiene to her country. The spread of medicine was to be her antidote to native superstitions. Kahesdee was anxious to continue her medical career that had ended all too briefly. She attached herself to Mrs Lyon for the best part of the medium's life. The spirit doctor knew it would require some soul-stirring experience, like the sorrow caused by her two-year-old son's death, to pave the way for this co-operative mission to begin.

You might ask what evidence there is for the existence of this spirit doctor. Margaret Lyon would reply that, using her faculty of clairvoyance, she has seen Kahesdee on many occasions, and gives a precise description of her. The unbeliever could still maintain that this is nothing but imagination. Nevertheless, there is confirmation of the medium's clairvoyance.

Once, when in London, Margaret Lyon telephoned Frank Leah, the psychic artist to whom I have already referred. They had never met, or even corresponded. Mrs Lyon did not give her name. Yet immediately Leah told her of the spirit presence of a Japanese doctor, stated specifically that it was a woman, and described her exactly as Margaret Lyon always saw her. A visit to the artist's studio showed that Leah had faithfully captured the likeness of the woman he had described on the telephone. This psychic drawing has pride of place in the room where all Mrs Lyon's healing is done.

Once again I am in difficulty because medical etiquette forbids me to mention the name of a doctor concerned in this cure. Margaret Lyon has lost count of the number of medical men who have consulted her for themselves, their closest relatives and for their most difficult patients. This particular doctor, after seeing a specialist, was told that he was suffering from tuberculosis. Because he was getting worse, he finally yielded to his mother's entreaties to consult Margaret Lyon. The worried mother, a Spiritualist, had badgered him owing to his deteriorating condition. The medium was even persuaded to visit the doctor at his home.

Through the entranced medium, Kahesdee disagreed with the specialist's diagnosis and stated that all she saw was a septic abscess on the left lung. She announced that she would not permit the lung to be drained, as had been suggested, maintaining that spirit healing could perform a cure. The doctor refuted all that Kahesdee said because of the specialist's diagnosis.

"We will argue about that after a pathological examination of the sputum has been made," was the spirit answer. A sputum test was made twenty-four hours later. The verdict was, "Non-tubercular". The first round had gone to Kahesdee. Even then the medical patient had his fears. He believed that he might have latent tuberculosis. Kahesdee was equal to the situation. She advised a guinea-pig test, which is considered to be final in these matters. After six weeks, the animals were alive and well. Kahesdee had won the second and final round.

In connection with this healing, there is a subsidiary psychic story that shows how confirmation can sometimes come in dramatic fashion. When Kahesdee gave her diagnosis, she described the spirit presence of the doctor's father, saying that, for the purpose of identification, she could see him holding a hypodermic syringe which he filled with a yellow liquid. "Did he specialise in vaccines?" she asked. "Yes," was the doctor's answer, as he admitted the accuracy of his father's description.

The communicator expressed pleasure because his son was in good hands, and added that he would acquaint his wife with that fact. "Note the time," were his last words to his son, "because this message will be confirmed." The doctor looked at his watch and saw that it was 6.45 p.m. All this, of course, happened in Glasgow.

The doctor's mother, in London, did not know that he was receiving spirit healing, although she had urged him to approach Mrs Lyon. It was a Sunday, and, concerned about her son's health, she wondered if she could obtain comfort at a Spiritualist meeting. She went to her nearest church, where Lilian Bailey happened to be the clairvoyant engaged for that service. The mother received the first spirit message. Mrs Bailey referred to the presence of the husband, who, once again, showed himself with his hypodermic syringe. He repeated almost word for word the message he had given to his son. The medium's spirit message was received at about 6.45 p.m. Two letters crossed in the post—one from the son to his mother describing the Glasgow happening, and the other from the mother to the son telling of the London sequel.

Another doctor, whose name I cannot mention, in confirming several cures by Kahesdee, stated: "I have seen X-ray photographs of men and women with gallstones. And I have seen the X-ray photographs taken after the patients were treated by Mrs Lyon. The stones had gone."

It is ironical to mention that a Church of Scotland

commission of inquiry into spiritual healing reported that its ministers should attempt treatments only in co-operation with doctors. My use of the word "ironical" is deliberate because Margaret Lyon is primarily responsible for the spiritual healing done under the auspices of the Church of Scotland's ministers.

The minister who has pioneered spiritual healing among his colleagues in Scotland is the Rev. J. Cameron Peddie. His church is in the Gorbals district of Glasgow, the heart of its slum quarter. When he heard of Margaret Lyon's healing successes, this minister brought his wife, who was troubled by fibrositis. Relief was instantaneous, and a cure speedily followed. The Peddies next brought their son, who was suffering from asthma and skin trouble. The complete cure was proved by his being passed A.I. for national service in the Royal Naval Volunteer Reserve.

"Do you think I could heal?" the minister once asked Kahesdee. She told him to go into the silence and meditate, and try to attune himself to the power that comes for healing.

The minister followed the spirit advice, and his healing faculty began to develop. The Peddies came many times to watch Margaret Lyon give healing. The medium often accompanied the minister on his visits to sick parishioners. Sometimes he brought sufferers to Margaret Lyon. Both in her home and in theirs the medium helped the Peddies to develop their powers. For eight years Mrs Peddie sat regularly in Mrs Lyon's weekly circle to help this unfoldment. Progress was so sustained that the medium frequently encouraged Mrs Peddie to treat some of the patients who came to the Lyon household. Mr Peddie has also appeared in public on Margaret Lyon's platform on the annual occasion when cured patients give their testimony.

There is apparently an apostolic quality in any gift of the spirit, in the sense that one who possesses it can stimulate it in another where it is latent. Just as Margaret Lyon was able to kindle the spark of Mr Peddie's healing, so he in turn was able to perform a similar function for other ministers. In this manner the healing has spread until there are now nearly a hundred ministers practising healing in Scotland.

One of them, a leading figure in the Glasgow presbytery, is the Rev. S. Smith, who first brought his mother-in-law for treatment to Margaret Lyon. This having proved successful, he came many times, bringing other patients. At one of these sessions Kahesdee told him: "You can heal, but take your time to develop." He followed her advice.

Margaret Lyon—or should I say Kahesdee?—had a great triumph when she was invited by the Rev. S. Smith to address Church of Scotland ministers on healing and to give them a demonstration. This took place in 1951 at Iona Community House, which is associated with the Church of Scotland.

More than one hundred ministers were present, including many who are now prominent in healing. The medium was warned beforehand that there would be a barrage of questions, but not one was asked. The Rev. S. Smith was in the chair, with the Rev. Cameron Peddie seated on the medium's left.

After a preliminary talk by Mrs Lyon, she was entranced and Kahesdee communicated. First, with great reverence, she asked for a blessing on the work that was to be done. "I have sought God's help," she said, "to guide me to a spectacular case, one of your own congregation that I do not know, for we still have some doubting Thomases among us." Kahesdee added that she wanted someone present who had become deaf through a blast or an explosion.

Finally a young woman in her thirties—she was accompanied by a friend who had made her understand the spirit request—put up her hand and said she might be the person to whom reference was made. "But you can't heal me," she added, "I have been deaf since 1943 when a land-mine exploded near the hospital in London where I was a nurse. I am stone-deaf. I cannot even hear the telephone bell ring."

Kahesdee replied: "I am not here to ridicule medical science, or to say what it can or cannot do. I am here to prove the gift of healing. Bring her to the chair." The ex-nurse came forward and was seated facing the audience. The entranced medium, who stood behind her, gave treatment while Mr Peddie, watch in hand, timed the performance.

Presently Kahesdee said to the ex-nurse: "Speak to your friend." The patient answered: "Are you shouting?"

"No," said Kahesdee, "you are hearing!" The audience knew that lip-reading was not the explanation of this instantaneous healing because the medium was behind the patient. "That took only five minutes," said Mr Peddie. "It could happen in the twinkling of an eye," replied Kahesdee.

Silence reigned, due to the profound impression created by this spectacular healing. "Are there any questions?" asked Kahesdee. The patient's friend broke in with: "No questions are necessary in the presence of a power like that." Then the ex-nurse spoke. "Why are you all silent?" she asked. "The days of miracles are not past." As a result of the healing she returned to nursing.

* * *

A slipped disc, that modern scourge, presents no problem to Edward George Fricker. If there are no complications, such as arthritis or sciatica, he cures a slipped disc in one treatment lasting a few seconds. I have seen many patients leave his modest house in Tottenham, North London, carrying as souvenirs of the healing the steel-ribbed corsets and belts which they had been told were indispensable.

In five years, Fricker has become a bright star in the healing firmament simply because he has obtained outstanding results with hundreds who have come to him as a last resort. It will give you an idea of the speed at which he works when I state that frequently he treats over two hundred, people in one day.

Healing is given in a small front room, which is about twelve feet square. Its most important piece of furniture is a piano stool, on which every patient is seated for treatment. The healer, radiant with vitality, and completely confident, never falters. He is both clairvoyant and clairaudient. His guides either give him the diagnosis, which is the quickest way, or occasionally the patient's troubles are reproduced on the medium's body.

The spirit healing band, says Fricker, is composed of former medical men, each of whom specialises in a different kind of ailment. It is the function of the spirit guide in charge to select the doctor best equipped to help the patient to be treated. The treatment, on the surface, is simple, for it consists either of laying-on of hands, or what appears to be rubbing the affected part.

The hundreds who flock to Fricker, and the thousands who write to him, do so through word-of-mouth testimony. They have relatives or friends who have been cured and so they seek treatment for themselves. The fact that Fricker lives somewhat off the beaten track is no deterrent. A sick man will always go where he thinks he can be healed.

Fricker's own story is as dramatic as many of his cures. Without realising it, he had been psychic all his life. Ever since he was a boy of five, he could remember hearing a voice which conversed with him but with nobody else. The voice always told him to say nothing about this phenomenon to his parents because they would not understand it. It is hard to believe, when you look at the robust Fricker, that he was a sick, weakly child, prone to illness after illness. He says that having suffered himself he is in a position to appreciate the sufferings of the many who throng to him.

His mother, whom he adored, suffered agonies for two years from cancer before she died. Watching her in pain, Fricker prayed that he might be able to heal others. One night, in his bedroom, he had a strange experience. A locket given to him by his mother, and which contained her photograph, mysteriously moved around the room. Fricker thought he was losing his reason. Neighbours, to whom, after some hesitation, he related this experience, asserted, because they were Spiritualists, that it was his mother seeking to attract him. They suggested that he should take an interest in Spiritualism.

Sometime later, he saw an announcement that Joseph Benjamin was scheduled to give public clairvoyance in a hall not very far away. Fricker decided to attend. It was a packed meeting. Halfway through proceedings, the medium described Fricker's mother—more perfectly, says the son, than even he himself could have done. Benjamin paused and said: "She is giving me an extraordinary name, one I have never heard before . . . Fricker. . . . Now she wants me to find her son." Unhesitatingly, Benjamin pointed to Fricker, adding that his mother wanted him to know: "You have a great healing gift."

This was the first indication of it that Fricker had ever received. It was one thing, however, to be told he had a gift, but it was another to find a patient on whom to try it. Then he remembered that his younger daughter, since birth, had been troubled with warts that disfigured her hands. He wondered if his healing could remove the warts. But what, he asked himself, must he do in order to heal? He just did not know the answer.

Then the voice which he had heard as a child, and which had been absent ever since, told him to put his hands on those of his little daughter, and to keep them there for a few seconds. Fricker followed the instructions, removed his hands—and the warts were still there. This, he mused, is the beginning and end of my healing. The next morning, however, the daughter came running excitedly to her father, holding up her hands to show that all the warts had gone.

His second patient was, it seemed, due to a chance encounter. At that time Fricker owned a factory—the demands of sufferers have since forced him to make healing his only occupation. He met a girl, whom he knew by sight, coming out of a nearby factory. She had just asked her employer to allow her to go home. Her migraine, which had troubled her for twenty-five years, was so unbearable that she could not work. His voice told him to treat her and she was cured instantaneously.

His sceptical brother sent him a third case, a man who was

forced for years to live encased in plaster. Fricker speedily cured him by following the directions of his voice. Those three cures launched him on his healing mission. The news spread rapidly, and the number of patients began to grow. It is still growing.

The trumpet has been levitated. Both hands of the medium, Leonard Stott, are held. Ectoplasm drapes his face, with one piece falling on his chest. And a 'spirit' hand is materialised.

Two streams of ectoplasm reaching to the floor envelop the medium's face and keep the trumpet suspended. The sitter is handling the ectoplasm. Medium is Leonard Scott of Philadelphia, U.S.A..

Chapter 18
DEFYING THE LAW OF GRAVITY

PHYSICAL mediumship is responsible for demonstrating the "impossible" so far as science is concerned. A table that floats in the air seemingly defies the law of gravitation, as does a trumpet suspended in space. This only means, however, that other laws are in operation which are responsible for these séance happenings. There is never any abrogation of natural laws, and thus there are no miracles. These "impossible" phenomena of the séance room are deliberately staged by spirit intelligences to meet the challenge of those who demand evidence that can be cognised by the five senses.

In the experiments, to which I have already referred, by Professor Crawford of Belfast University, he succeeded in photographing one of the methods by which a table is levitated. Ectoplasm, coming from the medium, formed itself first into a rod, and then into a cantilever, which, applied to the table, enabled it to be moved. Professor Crawford carried out a series of interesting and conclusive experiments which proved that the weight necessary to make the table rise was approximately equivalent to the weight lost by the medium at the time.

I have occasionally seen tables raised with their four legs off the floor. One Sheffield medium, with whom I experimented, regularly demonstrated this phenomenon. With one hand he vigorously rubbed the surface of the table. Then he placed both hands about nine inches above the surface, and the table slowly rose to meet his outstretched palms. Nobody was touching the table at the time.

With Jack Webber, a Welsh ex-miner, who lived in South London, it was a frequent occurrence for heavy tables to be levitated. Using infra-red photography, pictures were obtained of this significant phenomenon. The infra-red process also enabled me to obtain photographs of ectoplasm exuding from the medium and gripping one, and even two, trumpets, revealing the method by which the spirit operators caused these megaphones to move.

The secret of success at séances for physical phenomena is to win the co-operation of the guides responsible for producing them. When this is secured, and they know that you can be trusted, then the stage is set for success. That is one reason why sympathetic investigators fare better than cold-blooded researchers, who either inhibit the phenomena by their frozen attitude, or render the results nugatory by making it obvious that they regard the medium as a trickster whom they are going to expose. This failure to approach the medium as a human being is the reason why much of what is called psychical research becomes a blind alley. Mediumship is sensitiveness. The possessor of psychic powers feels more intently what others might easily shrug off. Thus the "convince-me-if-you-can" attitude, even when it is honest, is not calculated to produce phenomena that the inquirer wants to see. It is a human problem which must be faced.

If scientific research means the repetition of similar experiments under similar conditions, this is virtually impossible in the séance room, simply because the main factor is a human being, and a very sensitive one. On the other hand, it is possible, as I have done, to repeat experiments, not under precisely similar conditions, but to obtain comparable results.

When I saw with Webber a demonstration of how his jacket was removed and replaced, even though it was knotted and threaded, and he was roped to his chair, I asked his guides if we could photograph this impressive performance. I received permission, providing that only infra-red photographs were taken and that the exposures were made when signals were given through the medium.

The introduction of infra-red photography into the séance room has been a tremendous boon, for experience has shown that white light is harmful to the medium, unless it is used with the guides' consent and they make preparation to neutralise its effect. I have already described how mediums have been injured when, accidentally, white light was switched on.

For the purpose of my photographic experiment with Webber, he was securely roped to his chair. His arms were first lashed to each chair rest, then his legs were roped to the chair legs. I am quite familiar with the trick of straining yourself when you are being roped, so that by relaxing later you obtain sufficient slack to allow yourself to manoeuvre. I took precautions to ensure that this was not possible with Webber. Moreover, we had photographic evidence to show that the roping at the end of the séance was the same as in the beginning.

After lashing the medium to the chair, all the knots were threaded with black cotton, which normally would snap if there were any interference. Moreover the black cotton was also tied around a button in his jacket and knotted through a buttonhole. The slightest movement on the medium's part would have broken the cotton. Yet, at the end of the séance, all the knots and threads were intact.

The whole process of removing the medium's jacket and replacing it took fourteen seconds. Between the taking of the pictures we were asked by Webber's guide to put on the white light, so that we could clearly see the medium with his coat removed and seated in his shirt-sleeves. This was eight seconds after the séance had begun. Two seconds later, a third photograph showed the coat in the process of returning to the medium; it was half-way on Webber's body, with the sleeves partially back in their original position. The front of the jacket appeared to be semi-transparent, for the waistcoat buttons could be seen through it. The fourth photograph showed the coat completely restored to its original position.

Obviously the sitters were not responsible for this feat. None of them could have taken off the jacket without disturbing the ropes or breaking the cotton. In any case, every sitter linked hands with his neighbour.

I am not claiming that phenomena of this character are evidence of an afterlife, but they do demonstrate the existence of super-physical laws and of an intelligence that does not emanate from this world. The inference, therefore, is that it belongs to someone in a world of other dimensions. The intelligence, by its results, proves that it has the ability to reason. This type of phenomena is admirable for the sceptic, who is not interested in St Paul's aphorism that spiritual things must be spiritually discerned, but insists on witnessing spirit manifestations on a material level. Photographed demonstrations of the "impossible" were also obtained at séances with Margery Crandon of Boston, U.S.A. One of the results was called, "the greatest psychic exhibit in history". It proved the passage of matter through matter.

The experiments began at the suggestion of William H. Button, who was then president of the American Society for Psychical Research. Button, a keen researcher, was also a prominent Corporation lawyer. His legal mind had pondered the problem of producing evidence that would be in itself scientific proof of spirit power. Finally, an ingenious idea occurred to him, one that he propounded to Walter, Margery's dead brother, who acted as her guide.

If, Button suggested, two solid wooden rings could be interlocked at a séance, a feat that is normally impossible, they would be permanent evidence that could not be explained away, and would also reveal the working of a supernormal force. Walter promised to co-operate. The solid wooden rings were obtained at the next séance. In a few minutes they were joined, one inside the other. Button was so delighted that he asked Walter to repeat the experiment, which he did.

The jubilant sitters decided to acquaint Sir Oliver Lodge with the results. The famous scientist suggested that they should make the test even more stringent. It might be argued by a hypercritical sceptic, he said, as the rings were made from the same type of wood, that they were originally one solid block which had been cut into the shapes of an interlocking pair. To overcome even this criticism, Lodge offered to provide two rings each made from a different kind of wood. He supplied them, one of teak, and the other of hard pine, having photographed them before they were sent to Boston.

Walter was asked whether he could interlock these rings

of dissimilar woods. He did so, and the result, "the greatest psychic exhibit in history", was kept in a glass case. This led some of the sitters to produce pairs of rings made of differing woods, all of which were successfully interlocked by Walter.

Then a series of strange events occurred. Whether these were due to joking on Walter's part or not I cannot say, but it seemed as if he were playing games with the interlocked rings. Sometimes, in the séance room, sitters would see the rings looking as though parts of them had been eaten away. At other times Margery Crandon saw sawdust lying on the table and part of the pairs missing. Then the rings would be found broken or separated. Finally, there remained only the exhibit in the glass case.

When Hannen Swaffer visited the Crandon home, Button went to produce the prize exhibit. Alas, he found one of the rings broken as the result of a crack which he maintained could not have been accidentally made. This mysterious happening led Button to argue that there was "a law of frustration" at work.

"Walter has given us proof, time and time again, that this final evidence could be possible," he said, "but then something always happens to take it away. It makes me wonder." Is there such a law of frustration? I do not know.

Button, to illustrate his theory, produced a collection of apports which had arrived in the Crandon séance room. They were rock crystals and similar mineral specimens, some weighing several pounds. He told of an occasion when he was with Margery in the drawing-room car in a railway train. They were seated alone.

While he held the medium's hands, he asked Walter if he could produce an apport. One of these large rock crystals appeared suddenly on the table beside them.

Chapter 19
A SPIRIT SIGNATURE

MATERIALISATION is the greatest and the rarest form of mediumship. It involves either the complete reproduction of the physical body, or those essential parts of it that are required to achieve a temporary flesh-and-blood creation. What emerges at a successful materialisation séance is a living, pulsating, breathing, solid, conscious being who talks and walks, has heart and pulse beats, is warm and solid to the touch, and has blood or its equivalent flowing through its veins.

Louisa Bolt would hold a materialisation séance only once a year. Her slight, pale figure suggested anything but a materialisation medium. Yet it was at some of her séances that I saw my most outstanding results in this phase of mediumship. The séance I am about to describe is one that will always live in my memory, for a spirit promise was fulfilled that night. A materialised form stood in front of me and, as he said he would do, some months earlier, wrote his signature on a piece of paper which I held out to him.

As is usual for this type of séance, a "cabinet" had been made by curtaining off a recess in the room. Mrs Bolt, at her request, was roped to a chair in the cabinet. The red light was strong enough for me to see clearly the time on my watch and to be able to read the notes I was making.

A few minutes after the séance began, the four other visitors and I felt the cold psychic breezes which always accompany the production of these phenomena. Just as the cabinet, we are told, is used to store and condense the spirit power necessary to produce materialisations, so the cold breezes are said to indicate part of the process used by the invisible operators to obtain their results. The drop in the temperature is unmistakable.

From within the cabinet there appeared a small, white hand, which, we were informed, belonged to Ethel, the guide in charge of the phenomena. In a soft, gentle voice we heard her ask: "Can you see my face?" Then she appeared in front of the cabinet, a beautiful figure, clad in dazzling white raiment. I noticed, as I have frequently done, that although a red light illumined the room the ectoplasmic robing was snowy white. Neither did it reflect the red light.

Ethel insisted on showing us her strikingly beautiful face —incidentally, it bore no resemblance to that of the medium. Mrs Bolt is good-looking, but she would be the first to admit that her features could not compare in beauty with those of her guide.

Ethel asked each one of us to step forward and shake hands with her. Her hand was soft and warm. To all intents and purposes it resembled a completely formed human hand. When I shook hands with her, she allowed the drapery over her arm to brush me. I asked permission to handle this spirit robing, and it was readily given. I can only describe it as having a gossamer texture, far softer than the finest silk, and giving me the impression of feeling cobwebs.

One of the five visitors was Lady Caillard, whose husband, Sir Vincent, had promised to materialise. In earth life he was a well-known industrialist who had been president of the Federation of British Industries. I had not met him, before his passing, but had got to know his voice through hearing it at séances with Estelle Roberts and Louisa Bolt.

The voice I heard coming from the cabinet was similar to Sir Vincent's speech as I had heard it at other séances. The best testimony, however, came from his wife, who was easily able to identify it.

"I am doing my best," he said to her; "it all seems so difficult, because I am excited. I shall be with you in a moment. Let me get strong enough to bear the light." This clearly indicated that, in addition to the labours of the guides, the manifesting entity also has his contribution to make.

Next Sir Vincent addressed me, saying: "I shall keep my promise." A few moments later I heard him say to Lady Caillard: "I am quite ready. I am more than ready." In an earnest tone he prayed: "Oh God, give me strength."

Then he appeared in front of the cabinet's curtains. He was several inches taller than Ethel. I would have guessed his height as six feet. His features were completely materialised, even to his distinctive moustache. He called his wife by the nickname that she said he always used when addressing her. Then he turned to the side of the cabinet where there were some roses, brought by his wife, which had been placed in a bowl on a table. "My flowers," he exclaimed. With a clearly visible materialised hand, he took two roses out of the bowl and asked her to come forward. When she did so, he handed the flowers to her. "This is our final accomplishment," he said. First he took her by the hand, and then he embraced her.

Lady Caillard, a practising Roman Catholic, had started her inquiry into Spiritualism when her husband's passing left her grief-stricken with bereavement. Gradually the evidence for his survival had accumulated through many mediums and varied phases of phenomena. This, however, was the first time that he had materialised, to keep a promise he had made at earlier séances.

The scene that was enacted in front of us was one at which I felt I had no right to be present. This was a moving reunion between a dead husband and his living wife, the greatest of all human dramas, one charged with supreme emotion. The materialised Sir Vincent kissed his wife several times and, during their embraces, whispered words of endearment and encouragement to her. He had already told his wife, a very sick woman, at previous séances, that their reunion was not far away. He referred again to their forthcoming reunion which, incidentally, took place five months later, when she died.

When she returned to her seat in the séance room, Sir Vincent insisted on shaking hands with each one of us. Like Ethel's, his was a real hand. I know it was. When he shook hands with me, he slapped me with his other hand. They certainly belonged to a man! His hands were harder than Ethel's, which I had clasped earlier in the séance.

Sir Vincent announced that he would have to withdraw for a few moments inside the cabinet to get "more power". When he reappeared, Lady Caillard drew his attention to the fact that she was wearing on her wrist a watch which she had had specially made for him. By pressing a little raised catch, the watch chimed first the hours, then the quarters, and lastly the minutes, so that the time could always be told, even in the dark.

"Look, here is your watch," she said. As she held out her wrist, his materialised hand released the catch, and the watch chimed the time.

Then he asked me for my notebook on which to write

his signature, and so fulfil his promise made at an earlier séance. I had been taking notes in a "braille" notebook, a type I always used at séances because it contains raised lines and enables me to write in the dark if necessary.

I moved forward to the cabinet and proffered my notebook, which I had turned over so that his writing should avoid the raised lines. After he wrote part of his signature, he complained of the ridges, and asked for a plain sheet of paper. This I gave him. His wife handed him a pencil. I held my notebook with the plain sheet of paper on top of it. "Now we can see through a glass darkly, but then face to face," he said.

Then he wrote his signature. "Have I kept my promise?" he asked. I assured him that he had. Sir Vincent stepped right out of the cabinet and showed us that he was a fully-formed, materialised figure. "It has been a grand reunion," he said.

Even this was not the end of the séance. I was asked to step forward to see Ivy, a little coloured control who helps Mrs Bolt. Ivy asked me to hold a toy piano which she wanted to play. I knelt down to comply with her request. In my kneeling position I observed that she was just my height. I could see her black face, white teeth, thick lips and pink tongue.

Thus, at one séance, three distinctive, yet different materialisations had been made visible to us.

Louisa Bolt's psychic powers are responsible for the nearest to mechanical mediumship that I have seen. First came an apparatus, the Reflectograph. This consisted of a keyboard connected with a screen, on which illuminated letters appeared when the keys were depressed by spirit power. After months of experiments success was achieved,

A SPIRIT SIGNATURE 227

Infra-red photography records the levitation of a table, while the arms and legs of the medium, Jack Webber, are roped to his chair. All the sitters' hands are linked by each clasping the hand of his or her neighbour.

Infra-red photography takes you behind the scenes of a seance and shows the method by which unseen operators manipulate two trumpets, through which spirit voices are heard. The medium, Jack Webber, is lashed to his chair. A stream of ectoplasm from his mouth grips one trumpet. Another comes through his waistcoat to grip the second trumpet. The sitters are 'controlled' by each joining hands with his or her neighbour.

This psychic drawing is of Mr. J. P. Hutchinson of Windsor Crescent, South Harrow, Middlesex. His widow swore a declaration before a Commissioner for Oaths that the medium, Mrs. Coral Polge, never saw any photographs of her husband until after she had finished her sketch.

The nearest picture the widow could find was this snapshot of her husband dancing with her, It is given for comparison with the psychic drawing.

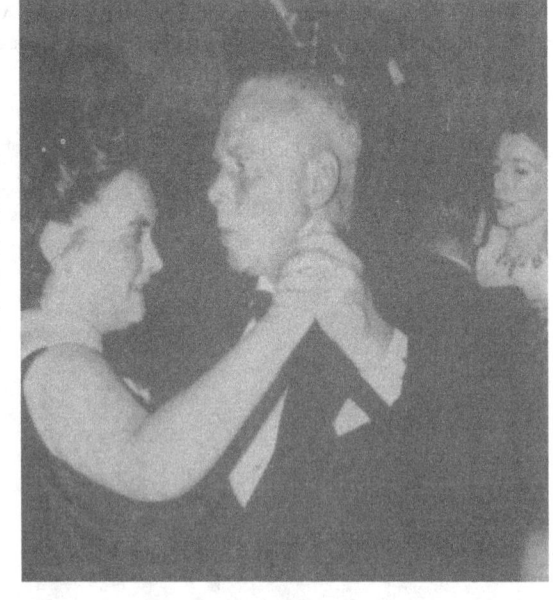

and in good red light. The medium was securely bound to a chair. From her there exuded a psychic rod which groped towards the instrument. From the end of the rod, a spirit hand materialised, operated the Reflectograph and spelled out messages.

Next came the Communigraph. This was in the form of a circular table with a glass top, through which illuminated letters were shown when spirit operators made contact between a pendulum and electrical points attached to a keyboard below the table. After each word was finished, a star was flashed on the screen. At the end of every communication a bell was rung. Two books were written on this instrument, every word being spelled by the communicator and recorded by a stenographer.

The final achievement involved sealing a Morse key so that it could not be operated in any normal way, and receiving spirit communications through it. It took eight years of development to reach the stage where spirit messages came in Morse code, in good red light, and with Mrs Bolt apparently no longer in trance, for she carried on a normal conversation all the time.

* * *

Had I not seen materialisations in the séance room I doubt whether I would have accepted some of the "miracles" recorded in the Bible. Many modern clergymen reject these biblical accounts of post-mortem appearances because they contend they conflict with scientific knowledge. It is strange that Spiritualism, which arouses the antagonism of those with very orthodox religious views, should provide the evidence that makes Bible "miracles" feasible because they are duplicated today in the séance room.

What is extraordinary is the fact that, although the Bible was translated by men who doubtless had no knowledge of Spiritualism, practically all their descriptions of what were undoubtedly psychic phenomena are in line with modern mediumistic happenings. Moreover, these Bible accounts comply with the conditions required by psychic laws as we see them operate today.

Dr Barnes, when he was Bishop of Birmingham, incurred the displeasure of clerical colleagues because he rejected the post-mortem appearances of Jesus and said they were myths. If he had witnessed, as I have done, a repetition of the phenomena which occurred in the Upper Room, he would have realised neither miracle nor myth was involved.

Jesus, according to the account, appeared in what was virtually a duplicate of his earthly body, one so solid that the sceptical Thomas was asked to handle it. In similar fashion, I and others have handled the materialised bodies of people who had been dead for years.

If the story of Jesus had ended with the crucifixion, it is doubtful whether anything more would have been heard of Christianity. Looking coldly at the Bible narrative, it is in-controvertible that the crucifixion represents Christianity discredited, its leading figure scorned and hanging between two thieves. One disciple had betrayed Jesus for thirty pieces of silver. Another proved to be a traitor, while all the rest fled in the hour of trial.

It was evidence, not faith, proof, not hope, that transformed the disciples into apostles burning with zeal to spread the new gospel. The evidence consisted in seeing that their leader had not perished with death. He had survived and, from the afterlife, gave proof of his continuing presence. That is the meaning of the séance in the Upper Room. It was similar psychic evidence that turned Saul, the persecutor, into Paul, the great propagandist. That is the meaning of what happened to Saul on the way to Damascus.

A knowledge of Spiritualism is the answer to many Bible riddles. Why did Jesus choose these twelve men to be his disciples? It was not for their calling, their education, their social accomplishments, or even their characters. My contention is that they were mediums, selected for their psychic talents, who constituted what Spiritualists would call the perfect circle. It is as true today as it was then that psychic gifts are not necessarily accompanied by spiritual, mental or cultural attainments.

Peter, John and James were what we would call physical mediums. Judged by the Bible narrative, their physical mediumship was not dependent upon Jesus but functioned even after his death. When psychic phenomena of a physical character were to be demonstrated, Peter, John and James were always asked to accompany Jesus. The superb example is the séance on the Mount of Transfiguration, where the pure air and stillness were ideal conditions for psychic manifestations.

Incidentally, nowhere in my reading of the New Testament do I find any accounts of psychic phenomena that are not in harmony with their present-day presentation. There are, for example, no daylight materialisations because, just as we have found today, white light is deleterious to the production of these phenomena. They always occurred at night or at dusk.

Let us examine this séance on the mountain, as described in St Luke's Gospel. As Jesus prayed, we read, "his countenance was altered and his raiment was white and glistening". Transfiguration is not an uncommon psychic phenomenon. I have frequently seen a medium's face become transfigured, by the ectoplasm built over it, until the features of a deceased person are clearly recognisable. And the "white and glistening raiment" is a perfect description of ectoplasmic robing.

Peter, John and James were "heavy with sleep", or, as Spiritualists would say, they were in trance. They awoke to find Jesus was communicating with Moses and Elias, who, of course, had been dead for many years. Then Peter suggested that they should build three tabernacles, one for Jesus, one for Moses and one for Elias. The word "tabernacle" could easily be translated as "cabinet". Peter doubtless had in mind the possibility of other materialisation séances being held on the mountain.

This séance provides the perfect answer to those who assert that psychic phenomena are condemned in the Bible. In support of their belief they usually quote texts said to have been uttered by Moses. If these texts are, as they suggest, condemnations of psychic phenomena, then Moses defied his own prohibitions when he materialised, with Elias, to Jesus.

St John's Gospel records that the first time Jesus materialised after his death, "when it was yet dark", Mary Magdalene, who knew him well, mistook him for the gardener. Such an error is incomprehensible without the psychic key. How could so striking and commanding a figure like Jesus be mistaken for a gardener? The explanation is simple.

The gardener must have supplied the mediumship

necessary for this first materialisation of Jesus. And because it was an initial appearance, the gardener's impress and personality were stamped on the materialisation—a not uncommon occurrence at séances today. It is not until Jesus calls her by name that Mary recognises who the figure is. Then she rushes to greet him, but is met with the injunction, "Touch me not". A similar cry is heard in the séance room when a spirit form has materialised for the first time, simply because the power is not strong enough to stand handling.

Later, in contrast, when Jesus appears in the presence of his twelve disciples, whose combination of psychic talents provides almost perfect power, not only is he clearly identifiable, but Thomas is invited to touch him so that his scepticism may be ended.

The moral I am trying to draw is the simple one that Christianity owes its existence to psychic phenomena that are similar to present-day séance-room happenings. Whenever I have gone to a materialisation séance, I have found myself comparing the demonstrations I witnessed with those described in the New Testament. I, like others, see in these phenomena a reason for accepting the Bible "miracles" which have caused thousands to turn their backs on supernatural religion. Thus the séance becomes a bridge where science and religion can meet, proving that science can be religious and religion scientific.

* * *

I have had many striking demonstrations of the power of the spirit, as the Bible calls it, with mediums in Britain and America when I have attended materialisation séances.

While on a lecture tour in America, I was invited to a séance in Pennsylvania, where I saw a materialisation and the medium at the same time, and proved it was not an hallucination by touching them both.

The medium was Ethel Post-Parrish, who, because it was the first time that I was present at one of her séances, invited me beforehand to search the room and the cabinet, the usual curtained-off enclosure. To please the medium, I made my scrutiny, although I knew that the evidence of genuineness would be in the results—as they were.

The room in which the séance was held was about forty feet long, and it was illumined by a good red light. Several forms materialised, and walked the whole length of the room. The outstanding figure to appear was Silver Belle, an Indian girl who said she was the medium's guide, mainly responsible for producing the phenomena. She proudly displayed a gleaming star on her forehead, and drew my attention to her two long, dark plaits. Her hair was entirely different in colour and texture from that of the medium.

Silver Belle came to me although I was seated at the end of the room, at the greatest distance from the cabinet. Taking my arm, she asked me to leave my seat and to accompany her across the room until we reached the cabinet. Then she invited me to go inside and make sure that the medium was there. Not only did I see Mrs Post-Parrish, I was told to touch her hair and to feel all down one side. All the time Silver Belle remained outside the cabinet. I was thus in the position to say that I stood between the medium and the materialised form, seeing them both and touching them both at the same time. When I announced this fact, Silver Belle took my arm again and walked back with me to my original seat.

* * *

It was Red Cloud, the guide of Estelle Roberts, who provided me with a demonstration that was just as impressive. It was a rare occasion when the medium gave a materialisation séance, a form of phenomena she did not often demonstrate. Before it, Red Cloud had requested that two luminous plaques and a red torch be placed in the séance room. These were put in the curtained recess which became the improvised cabinet.

Once again, it fell to my lot, at the medium's invitation, to examine the contents of the cabinet and make a thorough search of the room. To satisfy the medium's whim, I made my scrutiny and found nothing that was in any way out of the ordinary.

Estelle Roberts entered the cabinet and was soon entranced. It did not take long for psychic phenomena to be demonstrated. The two luminous plaques floated out of the cabinet and passed in front of the curtains. Between their phosphorescent glow I soon discerned the silhouette of a face. From the direction of its lips, I heard a voice which I identified as belonging to Red Cloud. I have heard it too many times not to recognise it.

At his invitation I approached within two or three inches of the cabinet. "Give me your hand," he said to me, while proffering his own. We shook hands. There was no doubt that I was not holding the medium's hand. The materialised spirit hand was strong and masculine, entirely different from that of Estelle's, which is slim and unmistakably feminine.

"Feel my hair," was Red Cloud's next request. When I

complied, I noticed, and felt, that his hair was long and silky and reached almost to where his shoulders would be. This was extraordinary because his medium's hair is short, crisp, wiry and inclined to be crinkly.

At least six times I left my seat and stood very close to Red Cloud's materialised form. Twice, to show himself as clearly as possible, he arranged for the light from the red torch to be focused on his features. It was a handsome face, with eloquent eyes. I judged his height to be several inches taller than that of Estelle Roberts.

* * *

I shall always contend that my friend, Helen Duncan, the materialisation medium, was the victim of a gross miscarriage of justice. When, during the war, she was charged at the Old Bailey under the archaic Witchcraft Act of 1735, some newspapers called it "The trial of the century." Obviously an Act which became law more than a century before Spiritualism began was not intended to apply to modern mediums.

Her conviction, and subsequent imprisonment, led Spiritualists to campaign, successfully, for the repeal of this Act, which, by being resurrected, implied that all séances were illegal, and thus jeopardised our religious freedom. In his war memoirs, Sir Winston Churchill has recorded that he sent a note to the Home Secretary complaining of the fact that in a time of urgency and peril so much time and money should be wasted on a "witchcraft" trial.

Counsel's defence that Mrs Duncan was a genuine medium, and his offer to demonstrate her powers of materialisation within the precincts of the court, were not regarded as legally admissible. The "offence" under the Witchcraft Act was pretending that she could conjure up spirits. Whether she was genuine or not was beside the point so far as this Act was concerned. Counsel for the defence was satisfied of her ability to demonstrate her materialisation powers at the trial, for she gave us evidence just before it opened that she was capable of doing so. Despite the strain of her ordeal, she willingly offered us an experimental séance which was remarkable in its results. Yards and yards of ectoplasm streamed from her, and billowed and flowed in swirling masses until even experienced Spiritualists like myself gazed with astonishment at the spectacle.

With Helen Duncan I have been privileged to see the growth of a materialisation inside the cabinet. Outside, I have observed the ectoplasmic forms as they gradually dwindled in size until they resembled small globes of light, and then finally disappeared as if sinking through the floor.

Inside the cabinet, I have watched ectoplasm exude from the medium's nostrils, mouth and ears in waving billows of luminosity that gradually solidified into the six-foot figure of her guide. Harry Price, a researcher who thrived on publicity, propounded the extraordinary theory that, instead of being a genuine materialisation medium, Helen Duncan swallowed yards of cheesecloth which she later regurgitated. To show how nonsensical this theory was, Mrs Duncan gladly submitted herself to X-ray examination. Price's "explanation" was that she had a secondary stomach, like a cow. The X-ray examination proved that both her stomach and her oesophagus were normal. Counsel for the defence at the Old Bailey tried to introduce the X-ray photographs as evidence, but these too were legally inadmissible.

More than once at Helen Duncan's séances, I was invited to handle some of the ectoplasm immediately after it had been produced. It was always bone-dry, and had a curious stiff "feel", proving that it could not have been regurgitated. I conducted an experiment that was conclusive in its result. At my suggestion, Helen Duncan, and every sitter at one séance, swallowed tablets of methylene blue. These had the effect of dying into a bluish colour the contents of all our stomachs. Yet when the materialisations appeared, they were their usual white colour.

Having given these examples of materialisation, I should like, in contrast, to furnish one that is exactly opposite—dematerialisation. Helen Duncan had a psychic gift which enabled her to read written questions placed in sealed envelopes, and to supply the answers. I tested this ability many times. Once I wrote a question concerning a woman with a most unusual hyphenated name, Bayley-Worthington. Naturally, I made sure that the medium did not see what I wrote, but she was able to repeat my question, including this uncommon name, and to give me a reply.

I happened to mention this phenomenon to Estelle Roberts, who, never having seen it demonstrated, expressed the desire to participate in such a séance. I arranged a meeting between the two mediums. I handed Estelle Roberts a sheet of paper on which she wrote a question which nobody else could see. She folded the paper and placed it in an envelope. This was sealed by her and handed to Helen Duncan.

Before attempting to "read" the question, Mrs Duncan followed her usual procedure. Slowly she rubbed the sealed envelope on her temple, and then at the base of her spine.

She said it was always necessary to do that before she could repeat the wording on the folded paper. Then slowly she exclaimed: "When—will—I—hear—from—my— . .?" Here, a puzzled expression came over Mrs Duncan's face. "It's gone!" she announced.

Estelle Roberts commented: "That is very good. You have read my question, all except the last two words." Still looking puzzled, Helen Duncan repeated: "It's gone!" Estelle Roberts assured Mrs Duncan that she was accurate as far as she had gone and, to confirm her statement, opened the envelope with the intention of showing the question she had written. Then we were all surprised, for the paper was gone! The envelope was empty. And the paper has never reappeared. Estelle Roberts told me that she understood the significance of this strange happening. She had asked a question concerning someone who had passed on, and recalled that Red Cloud had said she should not seek information concerning this individual until a certain time had elapsed, and that had not yet occurred.

Mrs Duncan's power of materialisation had another curious facet, in which a slate pencil would write without any seeming visible means of support. This was a phenomenon she never took seriously, and always had to be cajoled into demonstrating it.

The requirements were two slates, such as school children use, and a pencil. First I washed the slates clean and wrote a question with a pencil, making sure that the medium could not see what I was doing. Then I put the pencil horizontally between the two slates and tied them round with string.

Helen Duncan placed them beneath a table. She held one hand below the slates to keep them wedged and to prevent them falling. I heard the pencil make its usual scratching sound as an answer to my question was written. When the reply was completed, three distinct taps were heard coming from beneath the table. This was the signal for Mrs Duncan to produce the slates. When I opened them, there was a spirit answer written below my question.

Chapter 20
SUPPRESSED BY THE CHURCH

AN individual's religion usually depends upon where he was born. Those who defend with vehemence the doctrines they espouse as members, say, of the Church of England, would, in all probability, be equally as enthusiastic in advocating Hinduism if they had been born in India. No one really has an open mind on religion—and few are susceptible to argument. Mostly our religion is founded on what we were taught as children unless there are mental and spiritual upheavals in adult or later life.

The child accepts without question the religious teaching which it hears. Because its mind is resilient and plastic, the doctrines, expounded in all sincerity by adults, are accepted as literal truths. In time their repetition weaves them into the fabric of the subconscious mind, so that acquiescence has become almost automatic. Even in later years, unless there is an unheaval, questions on religion will produce almost mechanically the responses that were due to childhood training.

The older the individual becomes, the more difficult it is to discard religious beliefs to which he has clung for so long. This is especially true of clergymen. I once discussed this problem with the Rev. John Lamond, an Edinburgh divine who did not announce his Spiritualist convictions until very late in life. Obviously this was a question which had caused him much heart-searching. With a penetrating gaze, he told me that it had been one of his most difficult decisions to ally himself with Spiritualism that was frowned on by the "unco guid".

The clergyman's attitude to Spiritualism is similar to that of the doctor when faced with spirit healings. He is confronted with accounts of phenomena that appear to contradict everything he learned at college. Séance-room happenings do not fall into line with his theology. The clergyman's outlook is orthodox, and he may think his loyalty is involved. It is not surprising that he finds it exceedingly difficult to welcome what is claimed to be a "new revelation", through mediums whose phenomena are said to be similar to Bible happenings, which the clergyman regards with special devotion.

Whether he realises it or not, his theological training gives him a subconscious antipathy towards Spiritualism. Thus he cannot be expected to regard it dispassionately. There have been, as there still are, outstanding exceptions of clergymen who have championed Spiritualism. They were mediumistic themselves, or married into a mediumistic family, or for personal reasons became anxious to discover whether an afterlife could be demonstrated and received overwhelming evidence.

One of my great surprises was to be approached by a canon who told me that he was prepared to pay one hundred pounds if the afterlife could be proved to him. "Surely, as a canon, you believe it and require no evidence," I said.

"Yes, I used to believe it," he replied, "but I am not so sure now. I have lost my wife and I would like to know."

Although, by virtue of their calling, the clergy should be spiritual experts, their ignorance of after-death states is almost alarming. After all, they spend a great deal of their time preparing people for dying, and trying to comfort the bereaved. What too frequently stands in the way of their acquiring evidence of survival is a theological outlook based upon the acceptance of certain doctrinal beliefs.

The Church of England has had an inquiry into Spiritualism, one which lasted for two years. Its report was suppressed. Nothing more would have been heard of it had I not been responsible for publishing the main conclusions of its majority report. I have always maintained that if this report had been unfavourable to Spiritualism it would not have been consigned to the pigeon-holes in Lambeth Palace. While the commission was sitting, and even before its report had been made, a Lutheran clergyman wrote to the Archbishop of Canterbury for some information. This Swedish minister wanted Dr Cosmo Gordon Lang to tell him the attitude of the Church of England towards Spiritualism. The minister, the Rev. Martin Liljeblad, showed me, when I visited his Swedish home, the reply he received from the Primate. Said Dr Lang: "Spiritualism and spiritualistic services are not countenanced or encouraged in the Church of England."

Incidentally, the hostility displayed by Dr Lang is still in evidence today. This is indicated in the report of the Archbishops' commission on divine healing, which not only suppressed the evidence of cures offered by Harry Edwards, but seemingly went out of its way to present Spiritualism in the least attractive light.

The commission of inquiry into Spiritualism had its beginning early in 1937, when Dr William Temple, one of the greatest minds in the Church of England, was Archbishop of York. He was approached by Dr Underhill, then Dean of Rochester and later Bishop of Bath and Wells, and the Rev.

G. Maurice Elliott, a north London vicar with a great experience of mediumship. When they urged Dr Temple that the time was ripe for the Church to inquire into Spiritualism, he agreed. This was a broad-minded action. Only three years earlier, in a public lecture at Glasgow, Dr Temple had stated: "It is positively undesirable that there should be experimental proof of man's survival of death." This was a view he had held for many years. Despite his expressed outlook, Dr Temple approached Dr Lang and a committee was formed to investigate Spiritualism.

After a systematic inquiry, from 1937 to 1939, which included holding séances with mediums, the ten members of the committee issued their findings. Seven of them, the most influential representatives, signed a unanimous majority report. The remaining three—one was a bishop's wife, another a bishop's secretary—signed a minority report of a "sitting on the fence" character. Broadly speaking, the majority report was favourable to Spiritualism. I have its text in front of me as I write. Its signatories include Dr Underhill, Dr W. R. Matthews, the Dean of St Paul's, Canon Harold Anson, Master of the Temple, Canon L. W. Grensted Nolloth, Professor of the Christian Religion at Oxford, Dr William Brown, the celebrated psychologist, and Mr P. E. Sandlands, K.C.

I was unpopular with Lambeth Palace for revealing the contents of this majority report. Indeed, my publication caused such a stir in national newspapers that the Archbishop of Canterbury asked a leading Spiritualist to use her influence to suppress the press clamour on this matter. She was Mrs M. A. St Clair Stobart, chairman of the Confraternity, which sought an alliance between the

Church and Spiritualism.

Dr Matthews protested publicly against the report being withheld. So did Canon Gerald H. Rendall, who declared: "The ill-advised fulminations or injunctions of reverend 'Fathers in God', or the hush-hush policy which prompted the suppression of the findings of the Archbishop's Committee of Inquiry, reflect the timid clericalism which has so often been the bane of the official Church. Few realise the extent and weight of the resentment which action of this kind produces. Taboos on free discussion not only irritate: they give colour and excuse to the slogan, 'Clericalism is the enemy'."

When Dr Temple was appointed Archbishop of Canterbury, I tried my utmost to persuade him to publish the report. We had a long correspondence, but I made no head-way with him. The same Dr Temple who, in his crusading for social justice, showed that he was far in advance of his clerical colleagues, seemed to be almost a diehard in religion. And the same Dr. Temple, who was fearless in many pronouncements on controversial matters of the day, made sure that I could not quote from his letters by marking them either "Confidential" or "Not for publication". By making the report known, I urged on him, it would dispel the belief that the Church resorted to evasion and suppression rather than face up to truth. Dr Temple, who would not budge, even intimated that he had taken a foremost part in urging that the report should not be published!

Strangely enough, only two years earlier than our correspondence, Dr Temple wrote an article for the Daily Herald in which he said: "The most important political questions of the day are the questions whether God exists and whether man survives bodily death." Yet here he was, playing a leading part in withholding the evidence of man's survival. Could it be that as Archbishop of York, and later as Archbishop of Canterbury, his loyalty to his offices was the overriding factor?

It is part of my thesis that orthodoxy, not only in religion, but in every aspect of human activity, is a great barrier to the acceptance of new ideas. Orthodoxy inculcates a rigidity of mind which makes it difficult for new ideas to find lodgement. It is the real obstacle to the acceptance of Spiritualism by those who are members of any religious denomination.

I was able to publish the main conclusions of the majority report because at least one member objected to the results of the inquiry being buried in the archives of Lambeth Palace. Later, the majority report was printed in its entirety—not by the Church of England, but by Spiritualists. It is the perfect answer to those who argue that Spiritualism is anti-Christian. Here is one passage:

"It is often urged as of great significance that Spiritualism in many respects reaffirms the highest convictions of religious people, and that it has brought many to a new assurance of the truth of teaching which had ceased to have any meaning to them."

Another passage is even more striking: "It is clearly true that the recognition of the nearness of our friends who have died, and of their progress in the spiritual life, and of their continuing concern for us, cannot do otherwise, for those who have experienced it, than add a new immediacy and richness to their belief in the Communion of Saints."

In another declaration, the signatories affirm: "It is cetainly true that there are quite clear parallels between the miraculous events recorded in the Gospels and modern phenomena attested by Spiritualists. If we assert that the latter must be doubted because they have not yet proved capable of scientific statement and verification, we must add that the miracles, and the Resurrection itself, are not capable of such verification either." There was even criticism by the Church for being "altogether too cautious in its references to the departed".

The majority report ended by saying it was important that representatives of the Church should keep in touch with groups of Spiritualists. It is a pity, for its own sake, that the Church of England did not publish this report. After all, truth can never hurt real religion. The perfect ending to this chapter is the following quotation: "I think that one of the worst criticisms of our religious instruction is that we have created the impression that God was singularly active in one part of the world, namely, Palestine, until A.D. 66, but that He did not do anything anywhere else and has not done anything since."

Dr Temple wrote those words, which are a condemnation of Orthodoxy. Yet, when he was presented with evidence that revelation was a continuing process, even up to modern times, he helped to withhold this knowledge from the rank and file of the Church of England and from the world.

Chapter 21
THE IMPLICATIONS

I HAVE presented some of the evidence for the afterlife, which I regard as proven beyond all doubt. The evidence reveals that man, after death, is a conscious, intelligent, reasoning being, possessing memory, friendship, affection and love, and with the ability, given the right conditions, to guide loved ones left behind. So far as I can see, every type of evidence that would establish human identity has been demonstrated. It shows that man persists as an individual, with the traits, characteristics and idiosyncrasies that make one person different from everybody else.

All that can be demonstrated is conscious survival after death. Immortality, in the nature of the case, cannot be proven. There are no means by which it can be demonstrated that man will continue to live for ever. The logical implication of proved survival is that human existence will continue and not come to a sudden end. As we have had proof of the activities of beings of higher spiritual status than those possessed by man soon after his passing, it is reasonable to suppose that there is a law of evolutionary progress in the Beyond.

We are told that this is a process by which the dross is gradually eliminated and the pure gold of innate divinity finds increasing expression. Again, we are informed that the process is an eternal one, with a constant striving towards perfection. Each ascent, however, reveals another peak to be conquered. There is no finality in mental or spiritual attainments. The more you know, the more you realise there is to be known. There is no limit to knowledge. All this, however, must be regarded as speculation, but it is based on communications from evolved beings who have shown that they are capable of producing proofs of identity to satisfy the most cautious critic.

How do animals fare in this spiritual universe? There is as much evidence for the survival of domesticated animals as there is for humans. Dogs and cats have provided the greatest amount of proof of continued existence. Occasionally there have been psychic phenomena to establish the survival of a much-loved horse, a pet monkey and even a domesticated bird. I am sure, from the evidence I have received, that I will meet the domestic animals who were members of my family and who have died. They have proved their presence on numerous occasions. I am satisfied that all domesticated animals who have had an intimate association with man continue that bond in the hereafter. Indeed, for thousands of animal-lovers, heaven would not be heaven if the pets who shared their lives on earth were no longer with them in the Beyond.

It is individual consciousness that survives the grave. All animal-lovers know that their pets develop distinct individualities as a result of their close contact with man. It seems as if the association between human and animal either confers on the pet an individuality that it did not possess, or stimulates a latent individuality. The dog and the cat develop a "humanness" as a result of this friendship which they did not formerly possess. It may be part of man's contribution to the evolutionary scheme to confer this humanness on the animals who come within his care.

This humanness is a factor in survival. It draws the line

of demarcation between individual survival of domesticated animals and others which do not persist as individuals after death. It is possible to visualise a group survival of what, for want of a better term, one might call "the lower animals", as distinct from the individual persistence of a dog or a cat which gives evidence of almost a human consciousness. Beyond the grave even domesticated animals do not pursue the same path of evolution as man, at least, so I am told. The domesticated animal does not continue the process of perfecting its individuality. This need not disturb animal-lovers, for the separation may be hundreds or thousands of years hence. I have made the comparison in terms of years so as to give an approximation of a process occurring in a spirit world which is not subject to our dimension of time.

In dealing with the evolutionary law, I offer my views on reincarnation. This is a most complex problem which causes controversy even among Spiritualists. No point would be served in trying to gloss over the difficulty. The Spiritualist world is divided into two camps, pro-reincarnation and anti-reincarnation. A similar division is to be found in the spirit world, with the antis asserting they have seen no evidence for it, and the pros maintaining that it does take place. I think I could argue with equal force the case for and against rebirth.

The difficulty for the pros is their inability to provide, beyond shadow of doubt, evidence for a former existence on earth. I have read all the cases which claim to furnish this evidence, but none, in my view, measures up to the standard of being incontestable. There are always alternative explanations. The most simple, which conforms to facts already demonstrated, is spirit control. In mediumship, spirit control is shown to be a usual séance happening. It may well be that cases claimed as evidence of reincarnation can be explained by the individual being unconsciously controlled.

There are degrees ranging from inspiration, where the subject is unaware that he is the instrument of higher powers, to obsession, where a spirit entity has taken temporary or permanent possession of an individual. My friend Dr Carl Wickland wrote a book detailing his thirty years of séance experiences in which lunacy was cured by his wife's mediumship being used to dislodge the obsessing entity.

The not infrequent experience of people going to a strange town, at home or abroad, and being familiar with places they are seeing for the first time is not evidence that they have lived there in a previous life. It can be explained on psychological grounds, by the mind's awareness of the scene being ahead of the brain's recognition of it. Another explanation may be astral travelling, which is a well-established fact. It is possible to assume that an out-of-the-body visit may have been paid.

It is unfortunately true that reincarnation is accepted by a large number of people as a sop to a dreary, unadventurous life. It satisfies the ego to believe that in other times they were such glamorous figures as Roman gladiators or Egyptian princesses. Nevertheless, I am prepared to believe that in exceptional cases there is voluntary reincarnation, but not that it is a compulsory "law of karma". This "law" is propounded as an explanation of inequalities and injustices, and as a means of effecting compensation and retribution. But I fail to understand how an individual can come back to learn a lesson he had previously neglected if he does not know what that lesson is. I also do not see how any spiritual problems are solved by a man, who lived in abject poverty in a former existence, reincarnating with a silver spoon in his mouth.

Neither do I accept the argument that geniuses and child prodigies can be explained only by reincarnation. In addition to its hereditary strain every child is born with x, the unknown quality which is his spiritual heritage. The x is not the product of his parents or his ancestors. It is that portion of the divine spirit which incarnates and animates the body provided by the parents. Being divine, it has all the innate qualities of infinity. The child can just as easily be the spiritual superior or inferior of its parents, its grandparents or its great-grandparents. There is no simple equation between spirit and matter.

Geniuses and child prodigies may well be precursors of what evolution will produce in the human race in generations to come. Sometimes there is even a very simple explanation. My friend Florizel von Reuter was a child prodigy whose masterly violin playing was the sensation of Europe. He had appeared before all its crowned heads long before he was ten years old. His is an enthralling psychic story.

Florizel's parents had parted a few months before he was born. Mrs von Reuter was determined that her child should have a temperament that was entirely different from the one possessed by his father. Her ideal of what the unborn child should be was Paganini, the great violinist. While the child was still in her womb, she prayed intensely and ardently that Paganini should influence it and inspire it. Was her prayer answered? Is that the explanation of how Florizel became a child prodigy with his violin? Years afterwards, when mother and son became interested in Spiritualism and attended séances, mediums who did not know her story frequently described Paganini to them.

It is no part of my contention that Spiritualism will supply the answers to all man's problems. Certainly it furnishes some of them. By proving survival after death, it also proves that man is a spiritual being with a spiritual birth right and a spiritual destiny. Man is seen to be a spirit with a body, and not a body with a spirit—a distinction with a very great difference.

Man is not his body, though he identifies himself with it during the whole of life. "I am not feeling so well," he will say, when he really means, "My body is not feeling so well." Ludicrous as it may seem, the correct answer to a health question should not be, "Unfortunately I have rheumatism," but, "I am well, but my left shoulder has rheumatism." The reflection you see in a mirror is not you. Your birth certificate does not tell you who you are; it merely records the name by which your bodily personality is known.

Man, who has wrested from nature many of her profound secrets, who has plumbed the depths and soared into the heights, who has explored virtually every corner of the earth, who can destroy vast territories with one explosion; man, who is said to be the apex of creation, still has not found himself. His wonderful and fearful discoveries and inventions, instead of bringing him serenity, peace and tranquillity, have increased his fear and apprehension. He is more afraid of the future than ever he was. Materially, he may be prosperous; spiritually, he is bankrupt. His knowledge of the earth is massive; his ignorance of himself is appalling. "Man, know thyself," the ancient injunction, has still to be fulfilled.

The discovery of atomic energy has presented man with the greatest question-mark in history. He teeters precariously on the precipice, hoping for the wondrous boon that science may bring him, yet fearful that instead it may be the greatest catastrophe in which millions will perish. The problem arises because scientific discovery has outstripped man's spiritual development. He is not spiritually ready for the power that science has unleashed. Yet awesome and profound as these discoveries may be, the secret of life continues to elude the scientist. He cannot manufacture a microscopically minute object that is alive. How chastening is the thought that scientists can make an atomic bomb, but they cannot make a flea!

What is the difference between a living body and a dead one? Structurally, they appear to be the same. What, in a few minutes, has caused the heart-beat to cease? Why do the pulses no longer throb? Why is breath not being inhaled or exhaled? Why does rigidity overtake the limbs?

We die merely because that which animates the bodily frame has departed. The vital principle has been withdrawn. Without this dynamic the body and all its organs cannot function. This non-material principle is spirit, which is the essence of all life. It is impossible to define what is beyond language, but spirit is the stuff of life itself.

Psychic evidence reveals that man survives the grave as an individuated spirit. It is not death which confers a spiritual nature upon him. The body crumbles into dust, or is resolved into elements which no longer maintain a recognisable form, because the animating spirit has withdrawn to continue its purpose elsewhere. The body is the lesser; the spirit is the greater. The body is the servant; the spirit is the master. The body is the machine; the spirit is the individual.

Obviously that which has a limited existence of seventy, eighty or ninety years cannot be superior to the power which gave it life and survives its dissolution.

We are familiar with many of the physical laws which control earthly happenings. The séance room introduces us to a range of psychic laws which regulate the phenomena produced through mediumship. It is reasonable, therefore, to assume that there is also a realm of spiritual laws to control the spiritual aspects of being. All this indicates an infinite intelligence which is responsible for a law-governed universe in all its ramifications. Finite minds cannot comprehend infinity, but there emerges a conception of an infinite spirit as the divine architect of the cosmic scheme.

This is the God of the Spiritualist, not a deified man or a tribal deity, or, indeed, any anthropomorphic being. This is the God of all peoples, of all creatures, of the boundless universe, not the exclusive property of any religion or nation. This is the God incapable of favouritism, wrath, jealousy, vindictiveness, or any human weaknesses. "God made man in his own image," and man has been returning the compliment ever since. Man is not in the physical, but in the spiritual, image of God. The relationship is a spiritual one. Man here, and hereafter, is an integral part of this infinite spirit. He is born because a particle of it incarnates into matter and endows the body with life. He undergoes a variety of experiences designed to train and equip his spirit for the next stage of his existence.

At all times, every human being is united with God. This spiritual relationship is a fact in birth, life, death and beyond. It is an eternal union which cannot be severed. Because of this relationship, man is God in miniature. It is free will which decides, if he is normal, the extent to which he will allow the seed of latent divinity to flower. Potentially, man must possess all the powers of an infinite spirit. This, I believe, is the meaning of the words, "The kingdom of heaven is within." To which, of course, can be added, "So also is the kingdom of hell."

Man makes or mars his own destiny and creates his own heaven or hell. He determines his own spiritual evolution, which has nothing whatever to do with nationality, birth, station, wealth or profession. The natural law of cause and effect operates. Man is what he makes himself, by his conduct. Opportunities for the growth of character, which is really spiritual development, come to every individual. No one is in a more privileged position to render service than anybody else. To be unselfish, thoughtful, kind and compassionate do not depend on whether you are rich or poor. So far as character and spiritual attainment are concerned, we reap only what we have sown. The avaricious man cannot be a saint, for avarice cannot produce saintliness.

After death man continues his life at precisely the spiritual status which he had reached before leaving earth. It cannot be otherwise. It is impossible to have pretence, cheating or deception. The natural law cannot be thwarted. No one can pretend to be in possession of a spiritual development which he has not attained.

The standards of earth do not obtain beyond the grave where measurement is with a different yardstick. Here we can pretend to be different from what we really are because our true selves are seldom, if ever, revealed. We hide behind the mask of personality. Death strips away all masks, and reveals the soul in all its nakedness.

This natural law of cause and effect, or sowing and reaping, cannot be altered by death-bed repentances, by the recitation of any theological formula, by the administering of any so-called sacrament, however sincerely done or honestly accepted. No man, be he clergyman, priest or rabbi, has power to change the operation of natural law. Truly, "God is not mocked". The religious label, or lack of one, will make no difference. The acid test is only the life that has been lived. No recitation of words from books regarded as sacred can alter the working of universal laws, which are unaffected by attendances at church, chapel, temple or synagogue. What is regarded as religion by millions of people has a value, not because of what they believe, but only if it has inspired them to live a better life. It must be a personal and practical application to daily life. We are all individually responsible for what we do. Death will not transform sinners into saints, dullards into sages, or fools into philosophers.

The realisation that man is a spiritual being, which emerges from the evidence of the séance room, is a tremendous fact that ultimately will transform the whole earthly scene. It will give mankind a new sense of values based on an understanding of his place and purpose in the divine plan. Millions live lives of futility, chasing after shadow and illusion because they are ignorant of the purpose of their existence. Practically the whole of their attention is focused on bodies, with an almost complete neglect of their spiritual selves, which will be the enduring reality. If a fraction of the time, effort and energy devoted to our material natures were spent on unfolding our latent divinity, the world would soon be a better place. And millions would be living in spiritual light instead of darkness.

As it is, the majority of human beings die ill-equipped, unprepared and unready for the next stage of their lives beyond the grave. It is appalling to contemplate the thousands of uneducated misfits who die ignorant of what lies in store for them. They have failed to learn the lessons in the schoolhouse of earth.

Once you realise that you are a spiritual being you have a new scale of values and a totally different perspective. Fear and worry are banished when you are aware that no enduring harm can come to your real self. Besides, the knowledge that you possess a spiritual armoury, because of your divine relationship, teaches you how to tap some of that vast latent power within you, to provide strength in hours of weakness, guidance in times of crisis, and help when all seems difficult. This knowledge makes you realise that there are lessons to be learned in shadow as well as in sunshine, in pain as well as in pleasure, in sorrow as well as in joy, in storm as well as in peace. Each experience adds its quota and helps to make character, which is the eternal possession.

The greatest enemy in the world is materialism. This is the malignant cancer, with parasitical growths in all classes and nations. A knowledge of survival after death, with all its spiritual implications, makes belief in materialism impossible. Spiritualism is the antithesis of materialism. Spiritualism proves that the selfish individual is the one who must pay the price for his selfishness. The desire for power or wealth, no matter what suffering is inflicted in their acquisition, exists because the individuals concerned have no knowledge of the spiritual consequences. For a brief span power and wealth may bring false adulation and surface respect, but this is all very fleeting. Death brings a full stop to all the ambitions of dictators, misers, gluttons and hoarders. Just as goodness is its own reward, so selfishness brings its condign punishment.

In time, because of this new knowledge, antagonism, individual, national and international, will be replaced by cooperation and the desire to serve one another. Spiritual freedom will be enshrined as man's inalienable right because of his divine heritage. All the blots and excrescences which mar human existence and prevent the spirit from finding its full expression will be obliterated. Not only must the mind have full freedom, but the body, the temple of the spirit, has to live in conditions which are as appropriate to its setting as the casket of a brilliant jewel.

The whole of human relationships, in every aspect of being, will be altered by the appreciation of the spiritual necessities of life. Differences of colour, creed, race, language and nationality will be superseded by the prevailing knowledge of man's spiritual nature. In essence, the same spirit, though differing in degree, is within every human being in the world. This is an immortal and divine relationship that is even stronger than ties of family or blood. They will not persist, but our spiritual relationship will endure.

The simple truth is that God has made us all of one spirit. Whether we like it or not, the universal laws have so ordained it that the cannibal, the Negro, the Red Indian, the Aborigine and the members of every race, irrespective of the colour of their skins, are spiritual kith and kin. Spiritually, we are members of one another, all children in the divine family. This is, in fact, the spiritual United Nations.

Here are eternal truths which transcend all our physical differences. Killing cannot extinguish that spiritual relationship or end our responsibility to ourselves, or our duties to one another. The man who has been killed in battle still remains a spiritual fact that cannot be extinguished. War is thus seen to solve no problems; it transfers them only to other planes of existence.

Just as man will acquire a richness, dignity, lustre and nobility of life when he is aware of his spiritual potential, so a new order will dawn as these eternal truths are realised by rulers and those in high places. Then the visions of dreamers, reformers, pioneers and martyrs will have become realised and the kingdom of heaven on earth will be a living reality. Man will live in peace with his neighbour and himself. The power of the spirit will then be known in all its sublime majesty.

Chapter 22
POINTING THE WAY

I BELIEVE that it is part of the plan conceived by higher minds in the Beyond that spirit truths should be capable of demonstration to those who are ready to receive them. The story of revealed religion is one that shows the interaction of spirit and matter. The power of the spirit has always been at work, adapting itself, through the centuries, to the needs, understanding and capacity of its recipients. The Bible, like many other sacred books, is a testament to spirit activity. Whether many of its characters are called prophets, seers or mediums makes no difference. They were all the instruments of a higher power which, as it flowed through human channels, produced signs and wonders which were wrongly regarded as miracles.

Each revelation was tempered to the age and country in which it appeared. Always there was opposition from the upholders of the orthodoxy of the day, those who defended the letter, doctrine, dogma, creed, ritual and ceremony which were the obstacles to the acceptance of inspiration from a larger life. The new revelation usually came through a great medium, who first attracted public attention by the psychic phenomena that occurred in his presence. Then he would drive home the implications, the ethical principles which are the foundation of all world religions.

In course of time the leader died, and ossification set in. The original inspiration was forgotten, or buried, or overlayed by a new theological edifice. "The letter which killeth" had temporarily supplanted "the spirit which giveth life". So it became necessary for the cycle to be repeated again and again, as the higher minds found opportunities to present the eternal spirit truths which alone provide an understanding of life.

The position can be simply stated. Whatever happened in the past, in any part of the world, was due to the operation of natural laws. To alter, suspend or abrogate them implies a criticism of the governing intelligence which has to intervene because events are temporarily out of control through unforeseen contingencies. And that would mean that the Deity is neither omniscient nor omnipotent.

The laws of God are the same yesterday, today and for ever. Palestine is no more sacred than Britain. There can be no divine love for the year arbitrarily called one that is not equally available for any year in the twentieth century. In modern Palestine there is no evidence of the descent of spirit power that occurred there two thousand years ago. It is not the country which makes the spirit happening possible. Instead of "signs and wonders" in Palestine today there is the shadow of war. The trouble between Jews and Arabs is mainly due to differing theological ideologies. Similarly, this is the reason for the division in India between Hindu and Moslem. They are separated by creeds which cause "holy wars", if war can ever be holy. When theology supplants inspiration, the results are sterility and fratricide. Spirit, being the common denominator, unites people. Theology, with its belief in monopoly or special dispensation, creates barriers of strife and even hatred. How can theology, which emanates from the mind of man, compare with inspiration, which emanates from divine sources?

I see in the introduction of modern Spiritualism part of a

great plan to unify all religions and all peoples. Its evidence is that there are no Jewish, Protestant, Roman Catholic, Baptist or Hindu souls. When, at death, man discards his body, he also drops the scales from his eyes and begins to realise that spiritually he belongs to no nation, race or religion. When the implications of his survival dawn on him, and he appreciates how they differ from all his preconceived notions, his natural instinct is to share this tremendous news with those he loves, whom he has left behind, and who are as ignorant about it as he was.

Through all forms of mediumship which have developed in just over a century the means of communicating this knowledge are available. He does it first by proving his identity, so that the recipients are certain about who is com-municating. When identity has been established, then he can describe the conditions of his new life and its relationship to the ones he has left, to those who know they can trust what he says. In this fashion the revelation of modern Spiritualism is made known to increasing numbers as love speaks to love across the veil of death.

This is happening in millions of homes where the family hearth has become the altar. No ecclesiastical palaces are required, no cathedrals, no stained-glass windows, no vestments, no sacred images, no holy relics. This is not written slightingly or in disparagement. I realise that there is an aesthetic and emotional need in man that can be satisfied in surroundings where he finds beauty, tranquillity and, in thousands of cases, what he regards as his faith. But, with the greatest respect, none of this has anything to do with real religion. Praise, worship, liturgy, these may satisfy certain longings, but they do not necessarily bring man nearer to

God or give him a realisation of his spiritual nature.

As I see it, the plan is, and has been for over a century, to provide the ordinary man and woman with evidence of spiritual realities. f do not regard it as fortuitous that modern Spiritualism arrived on the earthly scene at a time when science began to develop its hold over man's mind. The Victorian era was one in which there was constant warfare between science and religion, and religion was the constant loser. Science would not accept anything that could not be demonstrably proved. Religion appealed only to faith, hope and belief. Triumphant, science became more and more materialistic; it would accept nothing unless it could be cognised by the five senses. Paradoxically, science has been compelled to move into the realms of the immaterial and to assert that the foundation of matter lies in points of power so minute that no instrument can register them, yet mighty enough to cause widespread havoc and destruction.

Religion without science encouraged credulity and superstition, the belief that priest craft possessed magical powers, and, in many lands, the fostering of illiteracy to perpetuate religious dictatorships. Millions were told that doubt was evil, that their immortal souls would be jeopardised if they read certain books which their spiritual masters decreed should be banned to them.

Religion without science has led to "holy" crusades, to the rack, the torture chamber, the inquisition in which heretics were condemned to die so that their souls might be saved. Religion without science has perpetuated the foolish notion that an infinite God can be the exclusive property of one Church, that one finite book can contain the whole of infinite truth, and that there are chosen people specially favoured by the Deity. Religion without science has asserted that faith is preferable to works, that salvation can be achieved only by the acceptance of theological beliefs. Religion without science has painted ludicrous pictures of a golden heaven reserved for the elect, and even more ludicrous pictures of a fiery hell for the doomed. Religion without science has led to bigotry and intolerance and playing upon fear. The religious implications of Spiritualism may not be discussed on the radio, B.B.C. television or any of the commercial television channels. This ban similarly applies to Unitarians and to Christian Scientists.

What has science without religion achieved? With nuclear fission it has brought humanity to the crossroads of destiny. Science is responsible for many boons. Its inventions and discoveries have enriched man's mind and given pleasure to his body. Communications have speeded up; the world has become smaller. Science has given man greater leisure, though he does not know what to do with the time at his disposal. It has enabled him to get much more quickly from one country to another, and from one place to another, though it has not shown him what to do with the time he saves. It has increased his expectation of life on earth. It has driven out many diseases, although new ailments arise, doubtless through the complexities of civilisation. It has multiplied the foods he eats, but the constant increase in population still presents the spectre of starvation in many lands.

Science without religion, unchecked by any ethical or moral considerations, has brought us the atom bomb. Scientists were accustomed to argue that the use made of their discoveries was not their concern. That position is no longer tenable. The discoveries are too massive and too fearful.

Science, which began by insisting on being materialistic, has been compelled to abandon its belief in the solidity of matter. Material solidity is an illusion.

I remember that twenty-five years ago, when Sir Oliver Lodge appeared as a leading witness in a case in which a medium was involved, the famous scientist, in answer to a question, declared that this was the world of illusion, and the spirit world was the reality. His reply was regarded with scorn. Science has now proved half of his contention, the illusion of solid matter. The other half will be demonstrated in the fullness of time.

What has all this to do with Spiritualism? I believe it is the bridge on which science and religion will meet and co-operate in the future. It is a religious science, and a scientific religion. Survival can be scientifically proved. Its proof has profound religious implications. When science and religion co-operate, as they were intended so to do, it will be a tremendous step forward in man's evolution.

Spiritualism, when fully understood, is unconcerned with any brand of theology. It is concerned with real religion, in the demonstration of spiritual facts which compel man to realise his relationship with every other individual and with the power which endowed him with life. With the evidence of spiritual realities as the foundation, science will work for the amelioration of humanity and for providing conditions in which the whole man, and not only his body, obtains the fullest expression. Religion, working in co-operation with science, will fulfil its function of fostering man's psychic nature so that he may be the recipient of even greater inspiration and revelation.

Thus man will work out his own salvation in the full

knowledge of what he is, what he is here for, and what he must become. His salvation lies in regeneration, in the recognition that he is a spiritual being, with a spiritual destiny to achieve. This is the great hope for millions who despair today. A war-weary generation, cynical, sceptical and perplexed, yearns for a philosophy and a religion suited to modern requirements. It has turned its back on old faiths, which it regards as exploded. The conventional and the orthodox teachings no longer appeal to the majority.

A Bible text is not the answer to doubts. The recitation of a creed, in which, too often, secretly, the clergyman no longer believes, is not most people's idea of a guide to life which mystifies and baffles by its paradoxes, perils and problems. Fearful of what the morrow may bring forth, they see themselves as corks floating aimlessly on an uncharted sea. And always there is the mystery of death to add confusion to an already chaotic scene. Science, they argue, has failed them. So has religion. Philosophy may speculate, but it provides no final answers.

Spiritualism points the way. It shows that God has not left Himself without a witness. It offers knowledge, backed by proof, to drive out ignorance and superstition. It shows that there is nothing to fear in death or in life. Man, the deathless being, need no longer live in darkness. The light of spirit truth is there to guide him how to live, so that when he passes he is filled with no regrets, because he will know his earthly pilgrimage was not in vain.

This is the modern revelation, accompanied, as of old, by "signs and wonders". This is the truth which every reasonable man can prove for himself. This is Spiritualism.

INDEX

A
Absent healing 20, 189, 195–196
Adams, Archie Emmett 45
Affinities 27
Animal survival 249
Anson, Canon Harold 244
Apports 166–169, 173–174, 220
Astral travelling 251
Aura 22, 77–78, 151
Automatic writing 18, 111, 114, 118, 120, 123–124, 126–127, 180–181

B
Bailey, Lilian 96–100, 207, 236–237
Barcynska, Countess 83
Barkel, Kathleen 166–168
Barker, Sir Herbert 197
Barnes, Dr 230
Benjamin, Joseph 73–74, 86–88, 212–213
Bennett, Arnold 122
Blatchford, Robert 136
Bolt, Louisa 222–223, 226, 229
Bradley, Dennis 101–102, 169–170
Brown, Dr William 244
Button, William H. 128–130, 217, 219–220

C
Caillard, Sir Vincent and Lady 223–225
Campbell, Chancellor R. J. 137
Canon of Bristol 111
Canon of Canterbury 111
Churchill, Sir Winston 236
Clairaudience 18, 75–76, 162
Clairvoyance 17, 21–22, 72–74, 76, 79, 81–82, 85–86, 101, 107, 110, 145, 151, 157, 161, 163, 205, 212
Communigraph 229
Cottenham, Earl of 52
Courteville, Robert 58–59
Crandon, Margery 124–125, 127–130, 218, 220
Crawford, Professor 125, 215
Cronin, A. J. 197
Cummins, Geraldine 111–114, 116–117
Curtis, Bob 181, 184–185

D
Deane, Mrs 177
Dearmer, Dr Percy 111
Dicyanin screen 22
Dingwall, Dr E. J. 120–121
Direct voice 43, 126
Dowden, Hester 113, 117–118, 123
Doyle, Sir Arthur Conan 143, 174–178
Duncan, Helen 236–240
Dyott, Commander George 59

E
Ectoplasm 18–19, 126, 166, 215–216, 232, 237–238
Ectoplasmic rods 43
Edwards, Harry 189–192, 195–197,

243
Elliott, Rev. G. Maurice 244
Ethel 223–225, 234
Evans, Mrs Caradoc 83
Evett, Iris 170, 173–174
Evett, Kenneth 170, 173–174
F
Faith healing 20
Fawcett, Colonel, P. H. 54–55, 58–62
Feda 140–142
Fife, Captain John 127–130
Fisk, Sir Ernest, 93
Flaubert 122
Fortune teller 17
Freud, Sigmund 197
Fricker, Edward G. 211–214
G
Galsworthy, John 122
George V 97
George VI 96, 99
Gibbes, Miss E. B. 112–113
Gibbons, Sir Walter 141–142
Granny Anderson 91
Grensted, Canon 244
H
Healing 20–21, 88, 143, 187–192, 195–200, 202–203, 205–211, 213–214, 243
Hopkins, Mrs 185
Horler, Sydney 184–185
Hughes, Helen 79–85, 90–91, 100–102, 107–110, 145–149
K
Kahesdee 204–210
Karma 251
Keiser, Mrs Ann 33–34
Kelly, T. John 34–35, 38

Kilner, Dr Walter J. 22
King, Mackenzie 45, 62, 79, 96–97, 99–100, 119, 153
L
Lamond, Rev. John 241
Lang, Dr Cosmo 243–244
Law of Attraction 27
Law of Karma 251
Leah, Frank 161–165, 205
Leonard, Gladys Osborne 136–137, 139–144
Liljeblad, Rev. Martin 243
Lily Dale 33–35, 38
Lodge, Sir Oliver 136, 219, 266
Logue, Lionel 96–100
Lyon, Margaret 202–209
M
Manning, Bessy 63–68, 70
Marconi 93
Materialisation 3, 18–19, 32, 126, 222, 232–234, 236–239
Matthews, Dr W. R. 244–245
Maud, Dr 111
Mazeeta 91
Mediums 10–11, 15–18, 20–21, 32–34, 38, 61, 66, 72, 74–75, 90, 92–94, 110, 124–125, 131, 133, 135–137, 139, 141, 143–145, 147, 149, 162, 166, 188–190, 217, 224, 231, 233, 236, 238, 242, 244, 253, 261
Mediumship 10, 14, 17–19, 22, 24, 26, 34–35, 39–41, 43, 45, 69, 72, 74–75, 80, 85, 88–92, 94–95, 97, 100, 112, 118, 124–125, 135–136, 142–144, 149, 151, 157, 161–163, 165, 175, 180, 182, 188, 199, 201–203, 215–216, 222, 226, 231, 233,

244, 250–251, 255, 263
Mesmerism 197
Miller, Mrs Caird 174–178
Mind reading 73-74
Morison, Professor D. 114
Myers, F. W. H. 112, 180, 182–184, 199–201
Myers, John 112, 180, 182–184, 199–201

N
Nicholson, Jerry 203
Nolloth, Canon L. W. Grensted 244
Nuclear fission 25, 265

O
Osterly, Dr. W. E. 111

P
Parish, Laurence 187, 199–201
Parish, Peggy 187, 199–201
Paterson, Professor W. P. 114
Peddie, Rev. J. Cameron 208–210
Phillpotts, Eden 122
Physical mediumship 215, 231
Post-Parrish, Ethel 234
Price, Harry 237, 258
Psyche 17
Psychic eye 75
Psychic faculties 17, 145
Psychometry 151–152, 157
Psychosomatic disease 21, 188

R
Rattin, Stephen 59–61
Red Cloud 39–41, 43–44, 47–52, 61–62, 64–65, 68–70, 76–78, 136, 170, 173–174, 181, 184–186, 235–236, 239
Red Indian guides
Reeves, A. E. 61

Reflectograph 226, 229
Reincarnation 250–252
Rendall, Canon Gerald 245
Resurrection 25, 247
Rhine, Professor J. B. 129
Richet, Dr Charles 18
Rimmel, Raleigh 54
Roberts, Estelle 32, 39–40, 42–43, 47–48, 54, 60–61, 63, 65–66, 68–69, 75–78, 131–132, 135, 152–156, 158–159, 170, 181, 183, 185, 223, 235–236, 238–239

S
Sandlands, K.C., P. E. 244
Sandys, Oliver 83
Scripts of Cleophas 111,114-116
Segrave, Sir Henry and Lady 45–53
Seton, Ernest Thompson 38
Shrenck-Notzing, Baron A. von 18
Silver Belle 234
Sleep travelling 27
Smith, Rev. S. 70–71, 209
Solar plexus voice 34-35, 38, 83-84
Spirit bodies 15
Spirit clothing 28, 76
Spirit forms 72, 74–76, 132–133
Spirit guides 17, 95, 188
Spirit healing 20–21, 88, 187–188, 192, 197–198, 200, 203, 206–207, 211
Spirit photography 18, 179, 182, 199
St Clair Stobart, Mrs M. A. 244
St Paul 72, 115, 218, 244
Subconscious mind 53, 66, 92, 94, 111, 241
Swaffer, Hannen 45–47, 96–97, 180–181, 220

T
Telepathy 10, 17, 22, 28, 53, 66, 72–73, 157
Temple, Dr William 153, 239, 243–245, 247, 257, 259
Trance 18, 35, 43, 88, 90–92, 94–95, 97, 100, 112, 126, 136–137, 140, 143, 202, 229, 232
Tyrell, Tom 74–75
U
Umbilical cord 19, 27
Underhill, Dr 243–244
V
Vibrations 14–15, 44, 77, 80, 83, 86, 151, 154, 169
Vivian, Dr Margaret 195–196
von Reuter, Florizel 252
W
Wallace, Edgar 180–181, 183–186
Webber, Jack 216–218
Wells, H. G. 122, 244
When Nero Was Dictator 117
White Hawk 166, 168–170, 173
Wickland, Dr Carl 26, 251
Wilde, Oscar 119–121, 123
Witchcraft Act 236–237
Woods, Shirley Ann 164–165, 220
Wootton, William Hedley 98
Y
Yeats, W. B. 121

Other books which may interest you

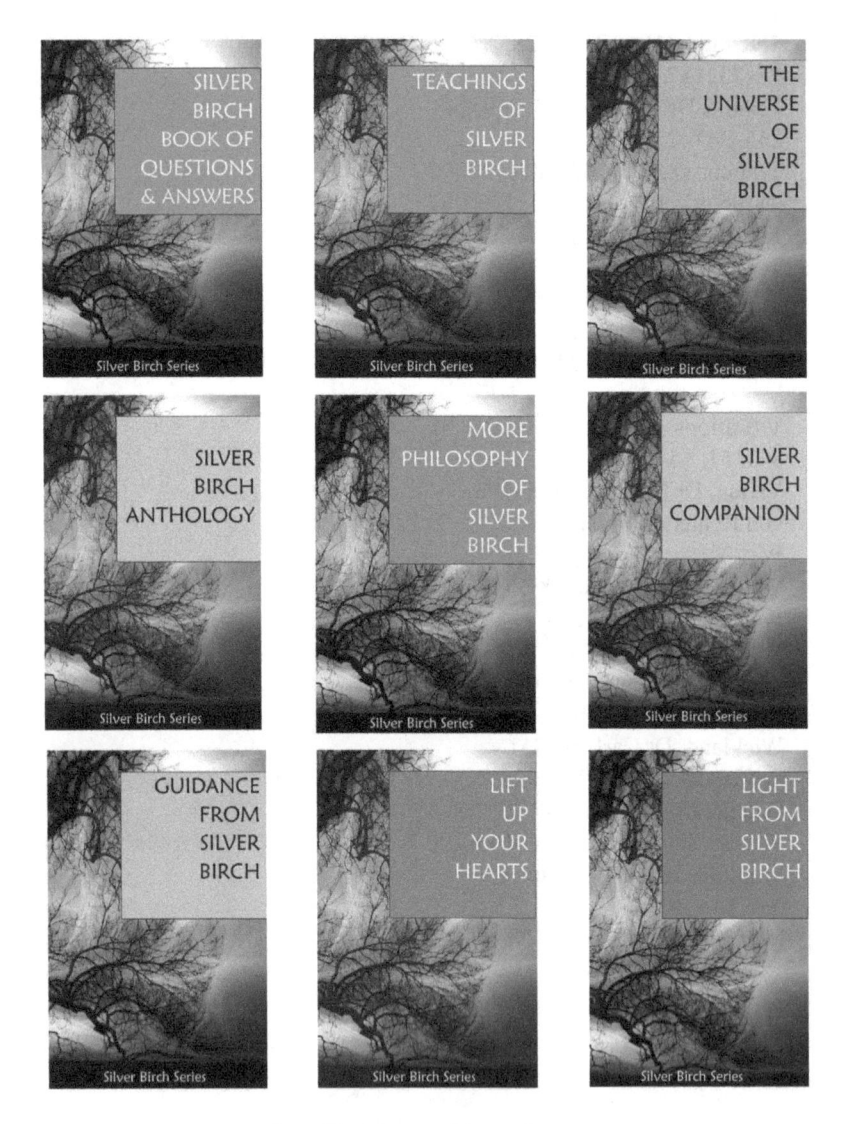

- SILVER BIRCH BOOK OF QUESTIONS & ANSWERS
- TEACHINGS OF SILVER BIRCH
- THE UNIVERSE OF SILVER BIRCH
- SILVER BIRCH ANTHOLOGY
- MORE PHILOSOPHY OF SILVER BIRCH
- SILVER BIRCH COMPANION
- GUIDANCE FROM SILVER BIRCH
- LIFT UP YOUR HEARTS
- LIGHT FROM SILVER BIRCH

Available online from
www.spiritualtruthfoundation.org

Other books which may interest you

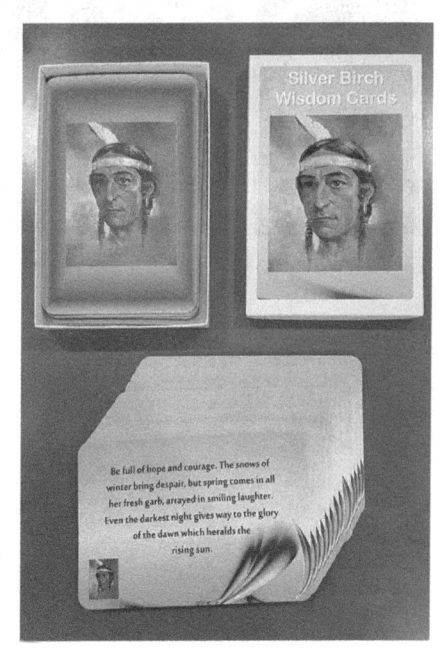

Available online from
www.spiritualtruthfoundation.org

Other books which may interest you

- SYLVIA BARBANELL — WHEN A CHILD DIES
- WHEN YOUR ANIMAL DIES — SYLVIA BARBANELL
- THIS IS SPIRITUALISM — MAURICE BARBANELL

- The Little Book of Silver Birch — Wisdom for Life
- The Little Book of Silver Birch — Wisdom for Healing
- The Little Book of Silver Birch — Wisdom for Animals
- The Little Book of Silver Birch — Wisdom for Challenging Times

- SOME DISCERN SPIRITS — By SYLVIA BARBANELL
- THE CASE OF HELEN DUNCAN — by Maurice Barbanell
- THE TRUMPET SHALL SOUND — by Maurice Barbanell

"In a moment, in the twinkling of an eye, at the last trump; for the trumpet shall sound, and the dead shall be raised incorruptible..."
I CORINTHIANS 15:52

Available online from
www.spiritualtruthfoundation.org